Walk with Me
to
Another Land

For Scott,

Who taught me so
much about walking!

Richard Zimmerman

Walk with Me
to
Another Land

A Narrative Approach
to Transitional Ministry

RICHARD P. ZIMMERMAN

WIPF & STOCK · Eugene, Oregon

WALK WITH ME TO ANOTHER LAND
A Narrative Approach to Transitional Ministry

Wipf & Stock
An Imprint of Wipf and Stock Publishers
199 W. 8th Ave., Suite 3
Eugene, OR 97401

www.wipfandstock.com

PAPERBACK ISBN: 978-1-5326-1554-2
HARDCOVER ISBN: 978-1-5326-1556-6
EBOOK ISBN: 978-1-5326-1555-9

Manufactured in the U.S.A.   04/14/17

To Annie

Somehow linked to life and a belief in God is the ability to face head-on the universal fear of change, to meet the inevitable changes that come with courage and resources, and to move out in creative ways to lose old images and old patterns and to embrace self-initiated change.

Bruce Larson, *The Meaning and Mystery of Being Human*

Contents

Illustration | viii

1   **Where to Begin?** | 1

2   **Walk With Me** | 12
    The Story of Ruth

3   **Why is Transitional Leadership Complex?** | 23
    Deuteronomy 34:9
    II Kings 18, 19

4   **You See the Need** | 38
    Nehemiah 1, 2

5   **On the Leading Edge of Loss** | 49
    Psalm 137
    The Story of Daniel

6   **Transitional Leadership and Transformation** | 65

7   **Where is the Hope? What is the Reality?** | 77
    Jeremiah 37, 38

8   **The Battle against Discouragement** | 85
    Nehemiah chapters 2–6

9   **Time to Refrain** | 98
    Luke 10:1–24
    John 20:21
    Leadership Narrative in Acts

10 **Moving toward Healing** | 110
    Mark 4
    The Story of Jonah

11 Leading through Shipwreck | 124
   Acts 27:1–28:14

12 Time to Say Goodbye | 131

Bibliography | 141

Illustration

Cartoon from *Puck Magazine,* 1881
On the threshold of office, what have we to expect of him? | 26

1

Where to Begin?

Eric stared out the window of his new office. A stack of boxes cluttered one corner. The shelves were mostly empty with the exception of a few odd remnants left by the previous pastor. He had plenty to do but he paused for a moment to catch his breath. He had successfully made it through the interviews and the job of interim pastor had been handed over to him. Now what?

He opened one of the boxes and started filling the shelves with the books in random order. *I'll rearrange them in some way that makes sense later,* he thought to himself. His eye caught the title of one of his favorite books on leadership as he pulled it out of the box: *Leading From The Heart,* by Robert Munger. He paused for a moment and flipped through the pages of the book. His eyes landed on a sentence that he had underlined when he read the book the first time. "While keenly aware of my limitations, I was confident that God would lead me through."

That felt right. Then he read on to the next sentence—not underlined—but now perhaps more relevant to his current situation.

"But I was not prepared for the deplorable situation that greeted me at the church."[1]

Eric could not remember what events greeted Munger in that narrative, but he could relate to the feeling. He was having a hard time getting a firm handle on what was really going on at this church. If he took reports at face value, the assignment before him was to lead the congregation through the transition after a pastor who was either similar to the Apostle Paul or David Koresh, depending on who was telling the stories. The loss of a beloved, long time pastor was bringing out the extremes in people. Clearly, many people were overreacting.

Just then the phone rang. An old friend was on the other line—an interim pastor who had led three different churches through pastoral transitions.

"How does it feel to be unpacking your books in another man's office?" his friend Brad asked.

Eric felt his chest tighten. "Well that's exactly how it seems, but how did you know that it would feel that way?"

"Hey I've seen it and felt it. That office is associated in the minds and hearts of the people of that congregation as the domain of the pastor before you. That is natural. The office is where they met on countless occasions for the most important events of their lives for the past several years. I'm not sure *every* transitional pastor has this feeling, but it is symbolic of what we do in this calling. We consent to enter into the challenge of living in the absence—the blank space—the place of a missing leader."

"Well, okay, but what do I do about it?"

"You need to take things like this feeling you are experiencing and give it a turn until you can see it from a different angle. Don't be the story. Instead, *see the story*."

"See the story?"

"Yes. People will constantly tell you that your significance—your identity really—belongs in the gap, the absence, and the negative space. You are the blank between pastors. You can't fight that, because, from a certain point of view that is entirely true. But your

1. Munger, *Leading From The Heart,* 109–10.

job is to see the story that is happening in them and from time to time, at just the right time, to help them see what their story is."

"That sounds good. Any suggestions for how I actually do that?"

"First of all, remember that it is never personal. You have consented to take on the role of transitional leader and that puts you into many interactions with people who are reacting emotionally to the experiences they are going through. But it is not about you; it is about the role you are in. So when you feel like you are being treated like a character in a story, take a look at that character. Pretty soon you will see yourself as part of the story, and you won't be dragged into the emotions of being that character. Does that make sense?"

"I guess so. It is yet to be seen if I can actually do it."

"True, and I believe all transitional pastors are only capable of doing it more or less. Still, that is the challenge. You can be most helpful if you are carefully attentive while being prayerfully aloof. I don't mean that you should be uncaring, you just need to maintain a certain emotional distance in order to really help them. One person sent me a letter thanking me for how I led them through their transition. He wrote, "I am especially appreciative of your *disinterested* interest in our congregation, all of us individually and our community." You have to find a way to genuinely care for them, while remaining free of the emotional traps.

Eric was truly grateful to have this advice from an experienced interim pastor, so he just listened quietly as Brad continued. "My way of keeping track of the many confusing events that happen is to maintain a story in my mind about what is happening in the congregational system. If the story is not accurate then you will be blinded to some things. So you need a story that can be easily revised. And maybe it needs to be constantly revised over the course of your time at the church. Your first question is, "Where does the story begin?" You can read through the congregational records going all of the way back to the founding of the church and even if they began many years ago you will probably detect the beginnings of interactions that are still happening in the church's story today. But more than that, spend time with people and listen to what they say for clues about the ongoing story."

Eric was eager to get started but he knew he was going to need more help as time went on. "This has been great. Can we get together sometime for lunch and talk more about this?"

Brad's voice sounded pleased when he replied, "Sure, I would love to have some time with you. I am sure you can also help me with some of the things I am going through in my congregation."

* * *

Most of the time pastoral ministry is like sailing against the wind. It takes skill, you feel like your heading against the flow, and the whole thing could get tipped into the water at any time. Now add the reality that a pastor is not a solitary skipper of an empty thirteen-foot sailboat, but instead is the leader of a whole boat-load of people who, while ultimately responsible for themselves, depend on the pastor for much of their spiritual lives. If the boat tips over a whole crowd of people will go over with it.

These are the dynamics of pastoral leadership under normal conditions. But in any kind of transition all of this is intensified. The winds are heavier, the storms more fierce, and the ship feels a bit more leaky. When the transition involves the loss of a pastor the congregation is thrown into an emotional turmoil. Sometimes circumstances or individuals force the pastor to leave. Sometimes a dearly loved pastor moves to a new congregation or retires. Whatever the circumstances, the congregation is thrust into a unique journey through change and loss. Yet the people of the congregation often do not identify or understand those emotions of loss churning under the surface. A transitional leader can make a tremendous difference in whether a congregation embraces a good future or gets stuck in troubled dynamics from the past.

Transitional or interim church leadership requires flexibility, improvisation, and persistent spiritual maturity in order to lead people through this journey. When faced with confusing signs, transitional leaders often crave greater wisdom about the unique dynamics of a congregational system in flux. How can one person with a limited set of gifts and skills adapt to the sudden and surprising needs inherent in diverse situations? In this book I will walk with you through the grief, loss, perseverance and hope presented in several biblical narratives as a way to deeply engage the dynamics of leading a congregation in transition. Having led multiple congregations through complicated transitions I have then gone back and reviewed the most important elements of any transition. Several biblical stories of how God used situational leaders to journey with people through significant transitions help to make sense of my experiences. It is my hope that these narratives, coupled with several case studies, my experiences, and other narratives, will make you ready to take action and to improvise as a transitional leader.

Now you may be wondering, *is it really that bad?* Or you may be thinking that the troubles facing a congregation in an interim are only intense if the pastor who has left was a disaster. In my experience, pastoral transitions are challenging regardless of whether the departed pastor was great or awful.

Consider the powerful impact of how pastors shape congregations. Either the strength of the pastor's leadership or the problems and disappointments of the pastor's tenure leave a mark, for better or worse, on the congregation. An interim or transitional pastor[2] is a specialist for the care and nurture of congregations adjusting to the new reality as they move from one pastor's leadership to the next. A change in pastors means a change in the most influential person in the congregational system. Change brings anxiety and anxious people crave stability. Yet the change of leaders forces the congregation to consider a whole array of other changes. These changes are often challenging. So the calling to be an interim pastor necessarily includes a calling to be a good steward of the congregations conflicting needs for both stability and change.

---

2. I will use the terms "interim pastor" and "transitional pastor" interchangeably throughout this book since both terms are used by various denominations and church traditions.

This voyage all takes place in a new reality of people's expectations—expectations based on past leadership, but increasingly, expectations have been intensified as the culture surrounding churches has changed. If pastoral ministry was like sailing a boat in days gone by, it is more like being the captain of a cruise ship in today's world. The consumerism pervading the attitudes of people means many church participants come with an expectation to be fulfilled by the activities of the church. Like cruise ship passengers evaluating the activities and destinations and looking to the captain to guarantee the safety of everyone on board, today's church participant often comes as a shopper asking *what's in this for me?* This is an inescapable condition of ministry in our context. Consumerism has invaded the thinking of virtually everyone in multiple unconscious ways. We see it in marriages, where people stay together as long as they are getting something from the relationship. We see it in the fundraising activities of nonprofit organizations as most appeals for funds involve a payback in some form for the "gift." We see it in our churches.

Consumerism is not all bad. It works pretty well to produce better televisions and cars as companies compete with one another to provide the best products at the lowest prices. But the constant appeal of marketing inevitably alters the outlook of every person participating in the culture. We all begin to ask *is this the best way to spend my money/time, or should I look for a more appealing option?* We begin to think we are *supposed* to ask that question all of the time before committing to anything.

This consumerism element is intensified when people are experiencing the stress of anxiety caused by change. The consumerist approach takes over thought patterns and creates an attitude of entitlement that poisons all interactions. G. Lloyd Rediger sums this up well. "A general sense of entitlement is growing in the church, as well as in society. Church members feel entitled to comfort and privilege. If a pastor does not please them, they feel free to criticize and punish."[3] So instead of floating as a great big ark of salvation, the church becomes one big cruise ship, primarily

3. Rediger, *Clergy Killers,* 20.

existing to entertain and to please. Congregations are glad to have a leader who produces the feelings and outcomes they desire. The trouble for leaders during a transition comes in the reality that not much of what happens within a transition—especially a pastoral transition—satisfies the felt needs and expectations of people.

Get used to the implied message: you could be replaced. And in fact you will be replaced—that is your unique contribution if you are the interim pastor called to fill the gap.

At its best, a pastoral transition is a time for turning back from a consumerist approach to church life—for returning to a more healthy understanding of the relationship between pastor and congregation. This will not be why most of the congregation thinks you are there. A transitional pastor gives a gift that no one is asking for: a fresh sense of the identity and mission of the congregation apart from whoever happens to be the pastor. This case study will give a glimpse of the type of work involved in such a calling.

Open or Close the Doors: a Case Study

Several years back the sanctuary had been remodeled to accommodate growth in the congregation as new members had swelled the numbers attending on any given Sunday morning. Part of the remodel included adding a fellowship/coffee area on the back of one side of the sanctuary. Someone had introduced a quite brilliant idea when the plans were formulated. Why not install a long set of accordion-style room dividers instead of a back wall in that area, so that after worship the room dividers could be opened and people could easily move from the sanctuary to the fellowship area for coffee? That way the fellowship area could also serve as overflow seating on special occasions when the sanctuary seating was not enough to accommodate everyone.

As an architectural design element this innovation seems like nothing but a good thing.

Those doors became the physical cause of some extended conversations for the transitional pastor. After a few months in the congregation this transitional pastor was confronted by some-one who wanted, "a moment of his time." Not knowing what the trouble might be he prepared himself for a multitude of possible issues. That initial conversation unfolded a puzzling controversy about those room-dividing doors. After worship is over, should the large dividers into the coffee area be opened, or should they remain closed? This initial conversation amounted to a report that one of the staff members of the church was engaged in an irratio-nal turf-battle, insisting for no good reason that the doors to the fellowship area must remain closed following worship.

The interim pastor next went to the staff member to get his side of the story. "There are dozens of good reasons why those doors have to stay closed," was the response to the simple inquiry about what was going on. "First, if you open the doors you make the whole sanctuary into one giant fellowship hall and it becomes too loud for anyone who wants to just sit quietly and meditate on the sermon after worship is over. Second, parents tend to linger in the area and they don't go get their kids, which means the teachers get stuck down in the classrooms and they never get a chance to have fellowship. Besides, we have never allowed coffee in the sanc-tuary. If you open those doors people will tend to bring their coffee in, creating too many opportunities for spills. Soon we will have stains everywhere in there. And also, the second service worship band rehearses in the sanctuary after the first service is over. They don't want those doors open while they are getting ready for the second service. And people in the fellowship area won't even be able to hear themselves think, let alone talk with each other with that kind of volume coming from the band."

All of that made sense. This hardly seemed like an irrational turf war. So what was the next move for this interim pastor?

The simplest response to this situation is to make a decree: the doors to the fellowship hall stay closed between services. This interim pastor took that path. It seemed like a trivial question: *open the doors or keep them closed between services?* All of the rel-evant considerations pointed to keeping the doors closed. So word was spread in a low-key way—let's keep the doors closed following the first service.

The next development came when an usher approached the interim pastor and said, "Are we supposed to open these doors following the first service? I was told they are supposed to be kept closed, but the associate pastor is insisting that they be opened."

The associate pastor was now a second staff member who had weighed in on the door issue without communicating to the transitional pastor. Something more was happening in this congregational system than a simple decision about doors.

Clearly interim pastors will do better to ask some questions before making decisions like this. Rather than being an unimportant nuisance question, the matter of the doors came to represent a whole universe of information about the ways people were negotiating the transition from one leader to the next. The previous pastor had been a remarkably capable leader—a strong and sensitive shepherd of all aspects of the congregation's life. In his absence, the passionate leaders of the various Sunday morning ministries of the church had stepped up their energy and initiative to improve the quality of their area in the life of the church. Those doors represented the clash of initiatives independently designed to get the church through the crisis initiated by the retirement of such a beloved pastor. The band was practicing harder and louder because they felt that music would be a key to church growth. Those in charge of fellowship wanted to improve that hour between services as it was crucial for building relationships. The Sunday school committee was having a hard time recruiting teachers because of the inevitable drop in participation that accompanies most pastoral transitions. Any new reason for members to be enjoying coffee and fellowship rather than teaching Sunday school made the dynamics of their ministry more challenging. Compounding all of that, a longtime pastor leads so smoothly that, ironically, congregation-wide decision making processes atrophy under very good leadership. In the presence of a good pastor the need for shared decision making processes diminishes. With the pastor retired those good processes for decision making and communicating needed to be fanned into flame.

After the initial whiff a new process was followed to answer the door question. Along with answering the presenting question a more patient approach emerged, addressing all of the subterranean conflicting interests in this congregation. A trivial matter of open or closed doors opened up new paths of conversation. Leaders reflected on how different people worship God differently. Committees engaged in theological conversation on the purpose of worship and the congregation's priorities for Sunday morning. New conversations began about how visitors are welcomed. The whole response led to a healthy reconsideration of how leaders are empowered to make decisions. As this interim pastor watched these conversations take place he sensed that new life was breaking forth in the congregation. What threatened to break out as a wildfire was transformed into more of a campfire of effective interaction burning brightly.

But not every pathway to new interactions is this smooth. The new realities in congregations undergoing a pastoral change are too much for some and they choose to leave the church rather than endure the uncomfortable changes. Congregations in transition often experience a heartbreaking parade of people walking out the door. Sometimes staff members resign or must be encouraged to move on. Sometimes longtime leaders simply take a step out of leadership even though they remain part of the church. Every one of these changes initiates a ripple of other changes. People who are already worn out by the feelings arising out of the loss of their pastor find themselves continually subjected to unexpected waves of change.

Powerful forces are at work as the church community is reshaped in preparation for a new pastor's ministry. This work demands attentive leaders who are always growing in their ability to lead in this unique era in the life of the church.

Fortunately, while the challenges of leadership are different than in the past, the resources available to meet those challenges are growing all of the time. Many books are available about the emotional systems of congregations and the best practices of leading groups through adaptive change. Narrative Theology also unfolds an insightful approach to these types of challenges. As I integrate the lessons of sociology and organizational leadership I will be using a narrative approach in this book to guide you along several lines of reflection as you improve your transitional leadership skill. The transitional pastor's first challenge is to quickly develop the ability to use narrative reasoning to place observed episodes within the narrative of the congregation's history. As we work with this narrative approach to transitional ministry we will consider case studies as examples of the dynamics of congregational interaction in transition. These case studies form our perspective for attending to narratives from the Bible as guidance for developing a wise approach to community transitions. Along the way a few other types of stories point to insights that could come in no other way than through narrative.

The beauty of a narrative approach lies in its power of broad application to any situation you might encounter. Once these stories are living inside the transitional leader intuititively knows a set of responses to certain kinds of situations. But more than that, your first unconscious reactions to every new challenge will flow from these stories. You will be a person who naturally walks with people from a place of loss and confusion to a new land of confident mission.

2

Walk with Me

The Story of Ruth

Naomi's story took place in a time of tremendous upheaval. For two hundred twenty years the central government was virtually non-existent. Without the powerful protection of a consistently unified army the Israelites were vulnerable. Neighboring countries would send raiding parties to take food, almost at will. Or worse, slavers might slip in and disappear with children, compelling them into slavery. While the chaos of the times shook nations, individuals lived out their daily lives, working and loving, scratching out a living, celebrating festivals and harvests, getting sick and dying, burying their dead and carrying on. Naomi's story forms the narrative in the book of Ruth, one of the most personal and practical books in the Old Testament. Walk with me through her story for a moment.

Naomi's husband, Elimelech, was a land holding farmer in Bethlehem. He had community standing and deep family roots. Like his ancestors, he cultivated the fields and raised his livestock. Before the famine arrived we might imagine him enjoying the quiet peace of home. His wife Naomi was delightful (that is what her name means), and the family was blessed with not one but two sons.

That picture was shattered when famine forced the family into exile in the land of Moab. The Israelites and Moabites were distant cousins and neighbors to one another, separated by the Jordan River. A persistent family feud sparked animosity and kept the rivalry alive between these two branches of Abraham's wide family.

It must have been a rather disgraceful thing that a free, land-holding farmer like Elimelech had fallen so far. Naomi would have felt the disgrace when she said goodbye to all of her lifelong friends and took the boys to Moab, where they most certainly would not have fit in. After the initial upheaval, Elimelech's family seems to have been accepted in Moab to some degree. Here the family found a home and some relief from their troubles. But life is full of changes. Elimelech died and Naomi was left with two unmarried sons. Not only did she lose the emotional comfort of her lifelong partner, she faced all of the challenges of survival without a husband to do his part. Poverty and the distance from friends compounded her grief.

It is a tribute to Naomi's tenacity that she was able to raise each boy to his wedding day. She managed to find wives for her two sons in spite of the difficulties that would have proven challenging for a women of her time.

After losing her husband it hardly seems that things could get worse. But then both sons died, leaving Naomi without a past or a future. The relentless pounding of tragedy was staggering. She was tremendously resilient, but when her two sons died she was beyond the point of keeping life together. Cut adrift with only her daughters-in-law beside her, this tough old woman from Bethlehem decided it was simply time to go home and admit defeat. In her shattered state she was forced to head right into the shining light of her disgrace.

Naomi and her two daughters-in-law had already set out on the road back to Bethlehem when Naomi reconsidered what she was making the two wives of her deceased sons do. In a moment of remarkably selfless thinking, Naomi's imagination began to paint a picture of the grim future ahead for these two young widows. Her grief and her need had pushed her out on the road, clinging to the two young women who reminded her of her sons. She now recognized how bad it would be for two young women with no husbands to stick with their mother-in-law and travel to a foreign land where they would not readily be accepted. She stopped right there on the road and pleaded with her two daughters-in-law to go back to the homes of their families. One of them did.

But for some reason Ruth decided to walk with Naomi into the empty future. Though Naomi passionately pleaded with Ruth to abandon her, Ruth decided otherwise: "Don't urge me to leave you or to turn back from you. Where you go I will go, and where you stay I will stay. Your people will be my people and your God my God. Where you die I will die, and there I will be buried. May the Lord deal with me, be it ever so severely, if even death separates you and me" (Ruth 1:16–17).

The narrative is lean on detail. It is not obvious what motivation pushed Ruth to make such a huge commitment. We might guess that Ruth was clinging to the memory of her husband who had died, or that Naomi was ordinarily a great person to live with and Ruth was hopeful that after grief passed that delightful person would return. Somehow through these awful circumstances Ruth had experienced the grace of the God of Israel and she deliberately chose to be adopted into that covenant. Ruth committed to walking with Naomi from a land of despair to an unknown land.

And this is my foundational image for all of pastoral ministry: to be a pastor is to engage in the action of walking with someone or some community of people from a place of despair and hopelessness to a place of hope. Ruth engages in the action of pastoral ministry in its simplest essential form.

Now Ruth has never been called a pastor as far as I know. But the image of her journey alongside Naomi highlights the narrative nature of our work as pastors. Our lives are given to serving people as they move forward according to a plot unknown to us. That plot is altered by the simple addition of someone who cares and who walks alongside. The inherent power of bending the trajectory of despair toward hope is possible because the God who created all things cares for each individual through the gift of pastors. All of the discreet areas of pastoral theology come alive within the framework of this image. Narrative preaching comes alongside of people in the middle of their troubles and walks them toward God's better future for them. Narrative leadership embeds change within the story of the church's movement from a scattered bunch of Christ-followers to a unified people bound for the promised land of the new community. Each area of pastoral work fits together in a highly textured whole under the guiding light of this simple image of the most basic pastoral action. In a multitude of ways, with careful preparation and constantly accountable engagement, a pastor walks with people from a place of hopelessness to unexpected place of new life. Ruth, a woman from Moab who refused to walk away from her hopelessly ruined mother-in-law, was engaged in the most basic and most enduring pastoral action.

I think of the couple that knocked on my door one summer afternoon. Their sobs made it impossible to even say a word for what seemed like at least fifteen minutes. But eventually they were able to croak out their story. Each of them had been raised in a family of faith, but as a couple they had drifted away from the church of their youth. They drove to my church from the hospital where their baby had been delivered stillborn. "We have walked away from our faith, and now we have nowhere to turn," they said.

I walked with them intensely over the next few days. Never really knowing if I was saying the right thing, always tentative in making my suggestions, I managed to plan with this precious young couple a memorial service for their baby. The questions were relentless. "Should we actually have a casket? Should we invite all of our family and friends and have a real service? Should we plan a service through the church in which we grew up?"

I cannot remember how I answered such difficult questions but I did guide them through the wrenching process whereby they made their own decisions and planned their service celebrating the resurrection to eternal life for their child who never took a breath. By their choice it was a small and intimate memorial service that

I led them through in our church's small chapel. When the service was over I invited them to participate in our congregation if their path led them to joining with us. They said they would think about it and that I may just get a phone call asking for more help in the future.

But I didn't hear from them. I wondered what the outcome of such a tragic loss might be for people who were teetering on the edge of making an adult commitment to their faith.

More than a year later I learned the outcome of their journey of grief. Though the loss of a child is forever an enduring source of grief, the intensity of that grief subsided as life went on. And the experiences of loss led them back to the church where they had grown up. They became very involved and were happy in their renewed commitment to their church. And they sent me a message to thank me for walking with them through their time of despair.

Pastors walk with people from a place of desperation and loss to another land. By God's grace it is a land of hope and new life. Transitional pastors are given by God to walk with people for a time, according to God's provision for the particular needs of the moment. A transitional pastor's role arises out of a particular kind of absence. The implications of this will continue to re-emerge throughout this book as we explore the singular nature of this calling.

Ruth's commitment to Naomi was expressed in the form of a covenant to walk from the land of despair to an unknown place. Watch what happened as a result of this covenant. After days of desperate travel the pair of widows walked into Bethlehem on the road from Moab. Naomi had been gone a long time, maybe about fifteen years, so it is not surprising when her old friends, the women of Bethlehem, greeted her by saying, "Can this be Naomi?"

"Don't call me Naomi," she told them. "Call me Mara, because the Almighty has made my life very bitter. I went away full but the Lord has brought me back empty" (Ruth 1:19–21).

"Mara" means bitter. After all she has been through, two words strain to fully carry the weight of what she is trying to say: bitter and empty.

When Naomi said that she was standing next to Ruth. Though Ruth and Naomi were together sharing the same conditions of poverty, loss, and fear, the contrast between the two at that particular moment is stunning. Naomi was finally home while Ruth awkwardly stood as the foreigner, beginning life over again in a strange land. Naomi had two sons, who grew to adulthood, and then they died. But Ruth had never had any children. Naomi's husband died after the two shared many years of marriage, but Ruth's husband had just recently died at a tragically young age. In comparison with Ruth, Naomi's life looks remarkably full.

Standing in silence, surrounded by her mother-in-law's dearest friends, Ruth may have been lonelier than at any other time in her life. But she quietly pressed on for the sake of taking care of Naomi.

Absence and emptiness drive much of what we do as pastors. For example, a pastor might look around the community and see that churches really are not reaching the single adults in the area. So with the vision of the fullness of God filling this absence in the community, a singles ministry is launched. Transitional pastors experience the odd reality of being both the symbol of the emptiness and the sign of an abundant future.

Just as a pastor looks at the emptiness in the community and sees what God's abundance might mean to the hurting and lost, so Ruth and Naomi could begin to sense possibility in the world around them. The two arrived in Bethlehem just as the barley harvest was beginning. The winter season of deprivation and hunger was just beginning to be over.

But what are two women to do, even if food abounds? They didn't own fields, and they didn't have the support of any men. Will their hunger be taunted by the plentiful harvest as they continue to waste away with nothing?

In Israel at that time there was a custom known as gleaning. Ruth and Naomi were in a vulnerable position with very little security or protection. The law prevented farmers from gathering up every last grain from their fields. Instead a small portion of missed grain was left in the fields to be gathered by people who were having a rough time (Lev 23:22).

Ruth and Naomi could stay alive by gleaning. But dangers still lurked on every side. Ruth was forced out into fields to search out the leftover grain after the harvesters had gone through, all the while avoiding being cornered alone by any of the men.

This is where Boaz entered the picture. Boaz was a distant relative of Elimelech, Naomi's deceased husband. Ruth did not know who Boaz was, but as she went out to glean she found herself working in the fields of this distant male relative. Boaz showed great kindness to Ruth because of the great kindness that Ruth had shown to Naomi. This story of despair began to show glimmers of hope.

Debilitating bodily pain often seizes those who suffer in grief when they think of their loved ones. At first Naomi could not do very much to improve the situation. In chapter five we will look more specifically at how people respond to all kinds of loss. But for now, simply take note of the lethargy that often strikes people when their world has been altered by some kind of loss. The once resilient and energetic Naomi could not seem to do anything. But Ruth could. And as Ruth worked to make their lives better, God provided encouraging events. As Ruth walked with Naomi from her place of despair, Naomi's sense of the world changed. Formerly Naomi could not even think of how anything might ease the pain of her hopeless life. Now she began to see beyond the despair.

And honestly, that is about all we usually hope for from a tragic story. The end of Ruth chapter two narrates the peak of our ordinary expectations when people suffer a devastating setback. Back in the hometown, with enough to eat and enough resources to expect they will not starve in the future, Naomi and Ruth have completed the process of recovery. But that is not the end of this story.

At this point a new word entered the narrative: "Redeemer." The word "redeemer" points to one of the Bible's most central themes, yet the word may not be big enough to represent all that is encompassed in this larger reality. Ruth and Naomi have hope because God has appointed a redeemer. In Ruth 2:20 we learn a vital piece of information. Boaz is a "guardian-redeemer" for Ruth and Naomi.

In the Bible the word "redeem" means to buy something or someone back which you used to have with you, but which, for some reason, has left you. For example, if someone had to sell some land the relatives were expected to buy it so that it could remain in the family (Lev 25:25). The same word is used for paying the price to free a slave (Lev 25:47–49).

In the days of Naomi and Ruth it was considered as an eternal death if a man died and had no living son. But here is where the concept of a guardian-redeemer could turn all of that around. A near relative could take the man's widow for a wife, even if this near relative were already married. The children born from this union would be the heirs of the man who had died. This way the life of the man who died is "redeemed" or bought back from death. This arrangement seems really odd to us. It does not make sense in our culture or to our way of thinking. But in their culture, even though Ruth was Naomi's daughter-in-law from another country, and even though the kinsman redeemer was the relative of Naomi's husband and not her own blood relative, still, the child born of this union was counted as Naomi's grandchild.

As Naomi moved from despair to hope an unforeseen change took place in the walk from one land to another. Beyond the mere restoration of some bearable quality of life, a new joy entered in. Ruth gave birth to a son who was regarded as Elimelech and Naomi's only grandchild, the heir to all of the family's land in Bethlehem. This was initially just an unexpected turn toward good news for one family. Over the next couple of generations this child became part of the royal line of David, and a thousand years after that the ancestor of Jesus (Matt 1:5 and Luke 3:32).

The Bible is filled with stories of people whose lives are lost. Then somehow, as the story unfolds, not only has the loss been re-covered but also something of God's creation has been redeemed. Redemption is that extra, unexpected gift transcending all natural expectation. The brothers of Joseph sold him into slavery. How could he recover from that? Our human perspective hears the beginning of that story and we hope that, by the end, Joseph will be rescued and restored to his place in the family. But we expect no more than that. And surprise! God uses the worst possible circumstances to eventually place Joseph as second in command over all of Egypt. When the family members are starving to death Joseph rescues them using the resources of Egypt at his disposal. That is recovery plus. As God redeems we always get a surprising extra bonus: recovery plus something more.

J.R.R. Tolkien unveils some of the nearly unspeakable mystery of redemption in his essay, "On Fairy Stories." He first creates a word, "*Eucatastrophe*" to point to what we feel when something happens in a fantasy story that turns the sorrow of a particular event into a greater joy than could be imagined in the beginning. "The consolation of fairy-stories, the joy of the happy ending: or more correctly of the good catastrophe, the sudden joyous 'turn' . . . is a sudden and miraculous grace: never to be counted on to recur." He then extends these observations to the "Christian Story." "The Birth of Christ is the eucatastrophe of Man's history. The Resurrection is the eucatastrophe of the story of the Incarnation. This story begins and ends in joy. It has pre-eminently the 'inner consistency of reality.'"[1]

Within God's redemptive activity it is often the case that someone consents to walk alongside in the grief, confusion, or in the ironic arrogance and self-sufficiency of that hopelessness. Surprisingly, the hopeless and helpless eventually arrive at another land—the land of God's redemption. A person who will walk alongside someone else on the way toward unexpected good news is a pastor. A transitional pastor is God's way of bringing redemption to a community.

My definition of pastoral action could have started with some of the great pastors I have known instead of with a couple of peasant widow women in the Old Testament. Or I could have taken Moses, Elijah, Peter or Paul as foundational examples of what it means to be a pastor. Yet the real barriers to a fresh understanding

1. Tolkien, "On Fairy-Stories," 81, 83.

of our pastoral calling are the many overlays of expectation that have unconsciously emerged over the years of the life of the church. I propose that we take this journey together, not beginning with the complicated picture that in our present day is mired in so much confusion, but beginning instead with the strands of narrative that clarify with precision the most basic elements.

I am committed to relentlessly considering these stories under the larger narrative of God's unfailing redemption. The work of a transitional pastor can be confusing. The needs of people are great. The responsibilities of preaching the message of the Bible accurately and loving people in the midst of their troubles can be daunting. Leading the development of a complex organization run mostly by unpaid workers can take up a lot of time. The pressures from the culture around us can so easily alter the trajectory of our mission in disabling ways. I still believe God uses transitional pastors for redemptive purposes.

In the narratives to follow I hope to create a fully formed picture of what it means to be a transitional pastor in a way that will guide you in your own church leadership story. Walk with me through these many twists and turns. As a result you will become a relentless symbol of God's redemption. If I tell these stories well you will see transitional pastoral ministry framed in unforgettable pictures of pastoral work. Narrative is often dismissed as the unnecessary decoration on serious theological thought, as though theology could be fully explained by discursive reasoning alone. I am asserting that many essential elements of pastoral theology can only be fully understand from a narrative framework that lays down foundational guiding images. Narrative is a way of thinking,[2] forming a theology of pastoral ministry that is a faithful representation of the essential task given to the church in the Scriptures.

Every year tens of thousands of congregations will undergo a change of pastors. Someone will be asked to lead each of those congregations through a transition. I am writing this in the hope that there could be excellent transitional pastors for these millions of people who have found themselves in exile and wandering in

2. Zimmerman, "The Fiction That Helps Us To Live," 2.

the grief, arrogance, or bitterness in the wake of their loss of a pastor. I hope you will walk with them to that other land.

3

Why is Transitional Leadership Complex?

Deuteronomy 34:9
II Kings 18, 19

Charles Guiteau walked into O'Meara's store on the corner of Fifteenth and F streets, examined two pistols, and bought the gun of the larger caliber. The date was Wednesday, June 8, 1881. This was not the wild west. Omeara's store was located on a quiet street in Washington D.C. That evening Guiteau took the gun to a wooded area down by the river near 17th Street and taught himself how to shoot, firing about ten rounds into a board. Once he was confident in his skills he went back to the boarding house where he rented a room. He cleaned the pistol and wrapped it in his cloak.

For several weeks Guiteau stalked the target of the assassination plot in the twisted tunnels of his mind and in several locations throughout Washington. The target was the President of the United States, James A. Garfield. In those times, with Secret Service protection for presidents still twenty years away, the amateur assassin was able to stalk President Garfield undetected for a couple of weeks. Then on Saturday, July 2, after enjoying his breakfast around seven in the morning, Guiteau meandered along the streets of Washington D.C. for a while before heading into the train depot. Newspaper reports had informed him that the President was scheduled to depart on the train that day.

Guiteau slithered into the rest room and pulled his pistol out of his hip pocket. Then he slipped out into waiting room. When President Garfield entered the area Guiteau stood up, approached from behind, and fired his gun twice. One round only grazed the President. But the other hit its mark, striking President Garfield in the back. At some point in the confusion Guiteau said, "I am a Stalwart, and now Arthur is president!"

The wounded President was taken immediately to the White House and the entire U.S. government went into crisis mode. Vice-president Chester Arthur was informed. The First Lady was rushed to the President's side.

Guiteau was arrested. He immediately handed over a packet of papers including a bizarre letter admitting he was the assassin.

The bullet did a great deal of damage. But the extent of the wound was not known at the time. Everyone was kept in a state of suspense, still hoping Garfield might somehow survive. For eighty days the President hovered between life and death. Those eighty days were the last on this earth for James A. Garfield. On September 19, 1881, he died.

Vice-President Chester Arthur took the oath of office at 2:00 o'clock in the morning on September 20 to become the twenty-first president of the United States. The entire country went into a period of mourning.[1]

Turn with me now, back in time some 3,300 hundred years and to the approach of the Jordan River from the arid lands to the east. Another pair of leaders faced a leadership transition. Unlike the transition from Garfield to Arthur, these two had the chance to plan for the coming shift in leadership. One of these two was near the end and he knew it. The other was just beginning and he also knew it. Moses and Joshua must each have been engaged in a searching assessment of themselves as leaders. As the people

---

1. Lossing, *Biography of Garfield,* 631–34.

of Israel drew near to their crossing of the Jordan River, Moses knew he was near the end. The Lord had made it clear to Moses that he would not cross over the Jordan and enter into the Promised Land. Moses was given the privilege of leading the people up to the lip of the Promised Land and no further. The leadership challenge of entering the land was to fall to Moses's successor, Joshua. Moses entered into his last eighty days reviewing his life and leadership, his faithfulness and his tragic failures. He must have been comparing his hopes and expectations with how the flow of life had turned out.

Those same eighty days would have been just the reverse for Joshua. Though he had been present for all of the great events of the past half-century, he was second in command and therefore responsible only to carry out the orders given to him by Moses. All of that was about to change. Moses was about to walk up Mount Nebo and never come back, leaving Joshua on the east bank of the Jordan with a whole lot of people and a very big leadership challenge. Yet his preparation could not have better, and this leadership transition was virtually seamless.

Chester Arthur had a tougher time succeeding James Garfield than Joshua had succeeding Moses. It certainly didn't help Arthur's cause that the perpetrator claimed to be carrying out this assassination for the sake of boosting Arthur into the White House. Guiteau was so obviously unstable that no one suspected that Arthur was ever part of the assassination plot. Still, it was not a good way to begin.

Puck Magazine, 1881
On the threshold of office, what have we to expect of him?

If you have ever walked into a leadership situation with a group that was never planning on having you lead them you will instantly recognize this body language. This cartoon from the day captures the attitude of the cabinet Chester Arthur was being asked to lead. It was a rough transition.

The adverse conditions for Chester Arthur's presidency began the moment Garfield was shot. Things were very unclear about who really was in control of the country during the eighty days when Garfield hovered between life and death. Garfield was lucid and everyone invested all hope in his recovery. So Arthur was never handed the keys to the administration until after Garfield had died. Once in office, Chester Arthur endured a series of resignations from the cabinet. In the end only one of Garfield's cabinet members remained. Much of Arthur's time was spent rebuilding his team. At the heart of his troubles stood a complex, unspoken, and unchangeable problem. No one had chosen Chester Arthur to be president. Everyone felt the loss of James Garfield. Most people were waiting for the opportunity to choose their next leader and move on to the next era.

As his shortened presidential term came to an end Chester Arthur declined the opportunity to run for president in the next election. None of us remember much about President Chester Arthur, though historians generally say he did a good job under the circumstances. Justus Doenecke commented, " . . . Arthur initiated little new legislation and was not an active leader, but he conducted the office with dignity and restraint . . . If the presidency as an institution did not gain much power, it did not lose much either."[2]

Most pastors begin with the general assumption that their new ministries will involve a transition of the Moses to Joshua type. In the rough and tumble of congregational life, typical pastoral leadership transitions are more of the Garfield to Arthur type. Not that pastors typically get shot in office, but smooth transitions are rare. Even when the leaders of a church carefully plan for a seamless transition from one pastor to another, complications often derail their efforts. Every leadership transition is complicated in its own way.

Yet people crave seamless transitions for the pastoral leadership of their churches. Church leaders often cling to a highly irrational tendency to believe their church will easily follow a smooth transition path against all evidence to the contrary. Somehow people believe it is better to hope all will be well than to bravely face the troubles, obstacles, or dysfunction at work in their church family. This is damaging. Spiritual health begins with telling the truth. While I never would encourage a congregation to wallow in their problems, pretending all of the snags will simply go away when a new pastor comes along often leads to living in the grip of an unhelpful mirage. Even in a relatively healthy congregation transitional leadership is more than merely blending the existing elements to create a beautiful picture of healthy congregational life. Rough transitions are common. Many leaders in the Bible began their work in the middle of complicated circumstances. Consider for a moment what you know of Elijah, Jeremiah, Nehemiah, John the forerunner, Peter, Priscilla and Aquila, and even Jesus himself. Is this not entirely a list of people whose pervasive reality is leading people through dramatic problems and persistent chaos?

2. Doenecke, *The Presidencies of Garfield & Arthur*, 183, 184.

Beginning in the middle of all of the chaos has a disproportionately large impact on the inevitable trajectory of ministry. Flip Flippen wrote a book on personal growth called *The Flip Side*, with a very intriguing subtitle: *Break Free of the Behaviors That Hold You Back*. He highlights the problem of beginning within preset dysfunctional conditions in his chapter, "Constraints Are Personal: My Story."

> My dad was married to another woman when he had an affair with my mother, and she became pregnant with me. My paternal grandmother (a genteel Southern ranch lady) threw a genuine Southern hissy fit when she found out an illegitimate grandson was on the way. She insisted that the right thing to do was for my dad to divorce his first wife and marry my mother, which he did.
>
> Now this is not the best way to start a happy family. Worse yet, I was at the center of the whirlwind, having "caused" all the upheaval the new marriage brought with it.[3]

It is not difficult to imagine how the plot of a story beginning with this kind of complication will go.

Pastoral leaders set out on a new ministry challenge intentionally setting in place the most important foundational conditions for long-term success in our churches. At least, that is what I did in the first three churches I served. But then, after eighteen years of pastoral service in those three settings, I was called to be transitional pastor in a congregation that was coping with the retirement of its beloved pastor of thirty-seven years while simultaneously making a shift to a new denomination. Over the course of two years I observed the struggle of people letting go of the way things had been in order to prepare for a new pastor. When that call was over I was called to be transitional co-pastor of another congregation with my wife, Annie. For the next two years we helped the congregation adjust to the loss of their founding pastor and helped them prepare for new leadership. In both cases the curtain was pulled back for me on the extent of how conditions are set

3. Flippen, *The Flip Side*, 180–81.

for pastors before they ever arrive. As with Flip Flippen's arrival in this world, a powerful story is already completely underway when a new pastor begins.

Transitional pastors work in this time between pastors to bring clarity and simplicity to the life of the congregation. Simplicity and clarity are important because the task ahead is, by its very nature, complex. A group of people with a diverse set of desires and expectations is looking to an unknown pool of candidates to find their next leader. Consider for a moment what is expected of this leader. The role of pastor is perhaps the most demanding leadership challenge in the world today from the standpoint of the diversity of skills required for success. All in the space of one week a pastor may be asked to review the proposed annual budget for the congregation like an accountant, hire a staff member like a human resources manager, fix an office computer like an IT professional, visit someone in the hospital like a social worker, assist in making life decisions like a hospital ethicist, teach a class like a professor, defend the nonprofit status of the organization like a lawyer, and then preach a sermon like no one else. Everyone understands that no one person could possibly be good at all of those things. Yet every church will have different members hoping the next pastor will be at least moderately good at every single thing on that list and more. Secretly there may even be people who are saying, "I hope he or she is good at golf."

So this task of finding the next pastor becomes a complex search for the person or people[4] who will represent the best balance of strengths and weaknesses for the congregation's mission in the world. Beyond finding someone who will be a good skill match for the mission of the congregation, it will also be important to find a good theological match, and a person whose philosophy of ministry lines up well within the *ethos* of the congregation.

This kind of complex search is best undertaken in an environment of calm. Yet in the absence of the leadership of an established

---

4. Most churches are looking for one person to fill their senior/lead pastor role. In the right congregation, under the right circumstances, a team approach could be the best choice.

pastor, churches within a transition find calmness to be an elusive state. This may explain why churches often lunge either for someone very similar to the previous pastor, or they overcorrect for past troubles by hiring their previous pastor's opposite. A staff member in one church once said, "When I saw the picture of the new pastor I said to myself, "Oh my goodness, they've hired Tom again." Tom was the previous pastor who had abruptly left after only three years. The new pastor physically looked so much like the previous pastor that some in the congregation were calling him "Tom" for several years after he came to the church. Other times congregations will lunge for their previous pastor's opposite.

All of these decisions flow from a collective frame of mind that is overly reactive to the past. Reactivity is the most natural behavior for congregations in transition, and also one of the most debilitating constraints for long-term congregational health. A transitional pastor is a shepherd of the spiritual maturity of the congregation within the context of upsetting change. That means finding ways of influencing the individuals and the group in the direction of several forms of maturity essential to a healthy outcome in the pastoral search. These forms of maturity include things like honesty about past hurts still swirling in the congregation, good boundaries, an awareness of the part the congregation played in past mistakes, and trust in the pastor search team. All of these things are subject to the influence of a transitional pastor.

Some church traditions have no official room for the kind of transitional leader I am describing. A bishop or a superintendent assigns the next pastor in a seamless transition. Or, conversely, in many independent churches a new pastor is quickly hired in the space of weeks or just a few months following the departure of the previous pastor with no real interim period. Yet in all cases the very same human dimensions of transition are at work. Under different practical arrangements the same dynamics of transitional leadership will apply.

Whatever agreements are in place for how the process will proceed, transition is primarily a spiritual matter. Though people will point out that finding a new pastor is a human resources matter, it is not *primarily* a human resources matter. Though transitional pastors definitely need to understand the sociological aspects of group behavior relative to leadership, this is not primarily a sociological matter. While congregational politics will play a huge role in what takes place, this is not a political process. Though many may want to use this as a time to bring change to a stagnant congregation, a pastoral tenure that begins as a protest movement is a doomed pastoral tenure. Having touch with all of the many ways of looking at the situation, a transitional pastor must resolutely view everything that takes place as primarily a spiritual matter. Believing the congregation was established by God for the sake of working out good purposes in the world, the congregation works its way through of the above dynamics in order to discern God's leading for the next leadership arrangement.

A leadership transition is an adaptive problem, not a technical problem.[5] A church cannot overcome the challenges presented by a leadership transition through working hard to apply effective solutions from its history. Instead the organization will thrive as people let go of the triumph and trouble of the past and embrace new ways of faithfulness for a new era of leadership. Paradoxically, change is necessary even if the main goal is to stay the same. A multitude of patterns, expectations, and interactions, must be dissolved and formed again in new ways. Everyone will say they are ready for change, yet most people will engage in behaviors that could only prevent change and protect the way things have always been. Moving on from the past and embracing the wide-open possibilities of an unknown future is more likely to occur under the calm leadership of a spiritually mature and skilled transitional leader.

So for the transitional pastor, spiritual practices become imperative, especially meditational prayer and reflection. What is true for all pastors is most acutely true for transitional pastors: if you are going to lead you must go there first yourself. Just like

5. For a practical discussion of the differences between adaptive and technical problems see "Distinguishing Technical Problems for Adaptive Challenges" in Heifetz et al., *Practice of Adaptive Leadership*, 19–23.

the people in the congregations I served, I have been frequently baffled by the complexities of the transition. Just like the people I have looked for comforting distractions to take my mind off of my anxieties. I have been guilty of hoping things will be smooth rather than confronting the sources of chaos.

The inner life of a transitional leader must be firmly anchored in the goodness of God, the reality of our tendency to estrange ourselves from God, and the unbreakable promise of a completely new creation because of the resurrection. One important theological feature of the beginning of Jesus's ministry is the radical break from the past, the giant step away from the *status quo*. And yet, Jesus is always asserted as a fulfillment of the way things were meant to be. Transitional leadership embraces these dynamics. We must be unflinchingly aware of the problems in the present and undaunted in our belief in a good future.

The answer to all of the complexity is the same in our time as it was in the time of Joshua and Moses. The people wanted certain assurances if they were going to follow the leaders. They wanted comfort, security, and an affirmation that the road to possession of the Promised Land would not be marked by great difficulty. Any promises made along those lines would depend upon realities completely out of Moses's or Joshua's control.

The only promises that cannot be broken are the ones that flow from spiritual realities. Pastors are constantly tempted to substitute our assurances for God's promises. And yet people need constant reassurance as they struggle with the many conflicting feelings inherent in the changes thrust upon them. Consider the moment when Jesus was sitting at a table, passing around bread and a cup of wine, and urging everyone to eat and drink. The mountain peak of this promise was followed by the abyss of the death of Jesus on the cross, which was followed by the mountain peak of the resurrection.

As transitional pastors we stand in front of a table with communion elements laid upon it, and we speak the words which call that fulfilled promise into the present. It is poignant that we do so knowing our time serving at that particular table in that particular community is limited. In this way a transitional pastor lives as a symbol of the transience of all pastors and the permanence of God's promises.

The reminders of the promises of God are everywhere. Do not look at the arms folded across the chest as a sign of rejection. Instead immerse yourself in every promise of transformation in the Bible stories that give life to the church, in the sacraments you celebrate with these people, and in every moment when life springs forth out of the difficulties you overcome together with them.

The story of King Hezekiah's interactions with the Assyrian empire in Second Kings 18 and 19 demonstrates these dynamics. I am, of course, not comparing the challenges of our congregations with Assyrian kings and their armies. The kings of the ancient Assyrian empire thought very highly of themselves. They felt themselves to be the center of the great pleasures of the gods. Assyrians dominated their world and sought to strike terror into the hearts and minds of all their enemies with fanatical fervor. Much of their art is devoted to graphically portraying the body parts of Assyrian enemies being paraded around on the ends of poles or displayed in other diabolically gruesome ways. The descriptions of their mighty deeds linger for an excruciatingly long time on the details of how they shredded and mashed the various body parts of their foes. Very few if any people in the history of the world could match the sheer brutality of the Assyrians.

So when King Hezekiah of Jerusalem was aching to provide himself with some help to prevent losing his skin, or any of the other body parts he had grown attached to, he entered into the mode of negotiator. For the price of all the silver and gold in the temple treasury plus the gold overlay on the doors and doorposts of the temple, Hezekiah attempted to buy the peace (2 Kgs 18:14–16). The price of peace was higher than that in the mind of the Assyrian king. He sent a large army to surround Jerusalem.

Hezekiah's imagination simply could not dismiss the gruesome thought of an Assyrian army sweeping irresistibly into the gates of Zion and tearing apart his precious people. Against the immense pressure of this threat Hezekiah had already gone heavily into the mode of strategic negotiator. He had already cut a deal with Egypt, hoping he might be able to protect the city with horses and chariots (2 Kgs 18:24).

If negotiating were the right mode, then Egypt would have been the right partner and a supply of horses would be the right prize. But negotiation was not the right leadership mode at that moment. Hezekiah abandoned negotiation and embraced the role of spiritual leader (2 Kgs 19:1). God sent the prophet Isaiah to redirect the thinking of those who felt negotiating for horses would be the answer. "Woe to those who go down to Egypt for help, who rely on horses, who trust in the multitude of their chariots and in the great strength of their horsemen, but do not look to the Holy One of Israel, or seek help from the Lord" (Isa 31:1).

It is difficult to criticize any king in this position who might want to have a few horses and chariots in his army. But that is exactly what Isaiah does. Can it be that we are barred from utilizing the potential resources available to us as leaders in order to achieve our goals? This passage gives some trouble to the reader.

I will admit my weakness. Initially I would have been solidly behind anyone who suggested Egyptian horses would be a great backup plan to the "trust in God" idea. After all, the Assyrians were some of the most brutal conquerors the world has ever seen. Does Isaiah really want to expose the city to the potential of getting overrun by the Assyrians? Sure, trust in God, but just in case, wouldn't it be a good idea to have some horses held in reserve?

No, it would not be obvious and easy to follow the prophetic word of Isaiah. The same is true of the challenges of spiritual leadership today. Leaders do not simply choose the wrong patterns of leadership out of arrogance or sloppiness. A wide array of forces—from fear to habit to ignorance—conspire to push leaders into the wrong mode.

But it does not have to be that way. Intentional leadership—the kind of leadership driven by thoughtful reflection and wise implementation of tested principals based on faith—responds in the freedom to flexibly choose the best mode of leadership for the precise situation at hand. If you can feel how tempting it was to rely on Egypt as an ally against the aggressions of Assyria then you begin to understand how forces around you and pressures and habits inside of you are driving your approach to leadership challenges. You probably do not even think about what leadership approach you are using; you just do what comes naturally. But the first natural inclination is not always the best choice. So what was the right leadership mode for Hezekiah?

In the story of Hezekiah we see a certain kind of leader tremendously challenged by a certain kind of problem. The situation reached Hezekiah's awareness *as a problem* because Hezekiah was fundamentally a problem solver. In fact, he was a fantastic problem solver. A careful review of the reign of Hezekiah reveals an amazing string of solutions to long-standing problems. For example, for hundreds of years Jerusalem was vulnerable to capture by siege because it did not have a reliable water source inside the walls. Hezekiah solved that problem by undertaking a difficult construction project involving tunneling through hundreds of yards of rock in order to channel a spring from outside the walls into the city. David never solved that problem, nor did the dozens of leaders who preceded Hezekiah. Hezekiah's primary leadership mode was as a solver of problems.

The Assyrian army was a problem without a natural solution. They were scary, and they were threatening Jerusalem, and nothing within the power of Hezekiah could come close to thwarting their power. But Hezekiah could not see that because he was a leader in perpetual problem-solver mode. He needed a prophet, Isaiah, to help him understand that the Assyrian army was to be confronted in the mode of spiritual guide. That certainly was not obvious. But it was correct. The Assyrian army was a sign pointing to the need for repentance. Hezekiah had to be flexible enough to set aside his most successful mode, and then take on an unfamiliar way of seeing the leadership challenge. He needed to marshal a completely different set of motivations, plans, actions and assessments than one who is in problem-solving mode.

This episode ended well for Jerusalem and Hezekiah. After a night of prayer Hezekiah looked out the next morning and the

Assyrian army had all been struck dead (2 Kgs 19:35). Historians and critics look for natural explanations for this miraculous outcome. However we choose to interpret the narrative, everyone agrees that Jerusalem had no natural way to defend itself against the overwhelming power of the Assyrians, and yet the city was spared right as Hezekiah abandoned all other modes of leadership and simply embraced his role as spiritual leader.

In light of Hezekiah's story, I see seven characteristics of the kind of transitional leadership that can counter the complexity of the challenges of congregations going through change.

1. *Reflective* This kind of leadership prayerfully explores the whole fabric of a situation in light of the specific needs arising at that moment in time.

2. *Chosen* Rather than reacting to the surface of the situation, leaders who can change modes choose a set of actions best suited for the deeper realities of the community's life and mission.

3. *Congruent* The inner strategies and plans in the minds of leaders must coincide with the outward actions. Good transitional leadership requires direct alignment of motivation, action and assessment.

4. *Consistent* Plans must be given time to work. The same course of action is pursued diligently over time without premature reconsideration.

5. *Principled* A deep sense of God's watchful eye pervades every decision. Actions are taken because they align with the most important truths facing a community.

6. *Action-oriented without being merely pragmatic* Leadership choices are carefully aimed toward accomplishing the mission of the church. Theories about how organizations work are evaluated based on their effectiveness in getting the job done.

Sell your books at
sellbackyourBook.com!

Go to sellbackyourBook.com
and get an instant price quote.
We even pay the shipping - see
what your old books are worth
today!

today!

When your old books are worth

We even pay the shipping - see

and get an instant price quote

Go to sellbackyourBOOK.com

sellbackyourBOOK.com!

Sell your books at

7. *Relentlessly faithful* More than merely sounding hopeful, a transitional leader must be completely set on the promise of a good future.

Complexity abounds in the swirl of a congregation caught up in the winds of change. In the middle of that complexity a kind of fixation on the simple goodness at the end of the long road will prevail. If that seems like a nearly impossible challenge, then turn with me to view the life of a man who faced what is possibly one of the greatest situational leadership challenges ever recorded.

4

You See the Need

Nehemiah 1, 2

Brad and Eric finally got together for lunch several weeks after Eric began his work as an interim pastor.

"Do you remember who the first person was to walk into your office?" Brad asked while they were waiting for the food to come.

"I think it was the music director. Why?"

"Well, I heard it said once that the first person who walks into a new pastor's office will turn out to be one of the most significant sources of trouble in the congregation."

"That sounds kind of crazy—almost like a superstition. Anyway, Mike didn't seem like he was being controlling or anything. He just wanted to go over the music for the next Sunday."

"Well, now, just go along with me for a minute. I really do think there is something to this. What if I said that among the first people to see you, one of them would turn out to be your most difficult person over the course of the transition? This person might appear to be a very supportive and dedicated advocate of finding the very best for the church. This person might appear to be a proactive and caring worker coming to talk with you as the transitional pastor in order to receive information about what is ahead for the congregation."

Eric thought for a moment. "Okay, if you are literally asking me who the first person was I can't say that my memory is good enough to be certain it was Mike. I talked to several people in that first week and I can't precisely remember the order of when they came to see me. But can you say that you literally remember the name of the first person who came to see you in all of your churches? And do you just starting preparing to thwart that person because he or she was the first person into your office?"

"No, not really. But let me tell you where all this is coming from. Being overly credulous I have believed in what appears on the surface over and over again in my initial interactions with people in churches, to my detriment. I don't want to become some bitter and hardened skeptic. So I have found ways to suspend my belief about the motives of people. I look for ways to be just a little bit reserved without thwarting good and honest congregational members. Because even if what I said may not be literally and always true, even if the first person into your office isn't literally the most troublesome person, frequently the most proactive people are working an angle to try to steer the life of the church in a certain direction. And they generally don't announce their intentions when they give a timid knock on the door and ask for a few minutes to talk."

Just then the food came so there was a pause in the conversation. Once they had prayed, Eric gave a bothered look and picked the conversation back up. "I have a hard time believing that people are taking advantage of me. It seems sort of sinister to doubt their intentions just because they are proactive enough to come right in and see me about something."

Brad said, "Yeah, I probably made that too dramatic. But look." He pulled out a pad of paper and a pen. "Just right now, write down a list of the people who made a point of coming in and introducing themselves in the first week, along with a short sentence about who they are and why they dropped by."

Eric took up the pen and jotted down a few notes:

- Mike, the Worship Leader came by to talk about songs for Sunday.

- Patty, the Secretary wanted to meet to discuss how she might coordinate with me for scheduling appointments when people ask to see me.

- Betsy invited us to dinner when we get settled in.

- Andre invited me to their Wednesday Bible Study.

- Chuck wanted to talk about pastor search committee formation.

Eric handed the pad over to Brad when he was finished. "Okay, that is typical I guess," Brad said as he scanned the list. "The motivations of each of those people might be entirely visible in the simple surface. Or each of those items might contain a plot to take control of the entire direction of the church. But look what happens when you literally write them down. First, getting them on paper represents getting some distance—getting some perspective. A transitional leader needs to be responsive and caring, yet detached from the emotional turbulence and control movements within the unstable system of interactions. You are not a participant in the emotional dance, you are a professional brought in to help support more straightforward and honest interactions. One way to physically reinforce your role in your own mind is to get the thoughts out of your head and onto a piece of paper in front of you that may serve as a record for yourself when you start to lose your perspective. But a second reason for actually writing down those first meetings is for your reference later on when your perspective on the motivations of people has grown deeper. In six months you may see that same first set of interactions in a different way."

Brad took what Eric had written already and altered the notes so that it now read this way:

- Mike, the Worship Leader came by to assert his control over the selection of songs for worship.

- Patty, the Secretary wanted to keep a tight rein on who met with me.

- Betsy invited us to dinner when we get settled in because she is feeling out of the loop now. Her best friend was the wife of the previous pastor and she used to have an inside track on everything going on in the church.

- Andre invited me to their Wednesday Bible Study. A disagreement about spiritual gifts is threatening to tear their group apart and he wants to know which side I will take.

- Chuck wanted to talk about pastor search committee formation. He does not want to be on the committee, but he wants to make sure he can agree with the direction they go.

"Do you see the advantage that will come if you can look at some of these things on paper? See, I don't even know these people. I have no clue of what they are really all about. I completely invented those manipulative reasons for why they may have been coming to see you. But if you can look at it on paper, if you can see a trend, you will start to see the story unfolding. Because if any of these people are trying to take advantage of you, they are not really doing it to *you*. Whatever their motivations were, those motivations were already in place when they met you. See? And if you can make it less about you, then you will be more effective in leading them towards better ways of interacting with one another."

Eric was a little surprised by all of this and so he paused to think it all over. "I see what you mean. Deep down I wondered what motivations were behind those visits, but I didn't think it was . . ." he was groping for the right word. " . . . I didn't think it was *fair* for me to question their motives like that."

Brad smiled. "I have always loved that about you, Eric. You are a highly principled guy. So don't ever change. But still you need to move toward becoming more wise and watchful. Now look back at my list one more time. None of the motivations I invented are really sinister. But all of those motivations have the potential to move those people toward highly disruptive actions. Don't *disbelieve* people. Just don't be so late in seeing the patterns. If you are constantly behind you will put yourself at a disadvantage in your leadership."

*　*　*

A transitional pastor is a situational leader brought in from outside the local context for a specific purpose. In my denomination the transitional pastor is ordinarily slated to leave after a new pastor is found, but this is not required and sometimes the transitional pastor moves into the role of pastor. In many ways the situation is similar to what Nehemiah faced in the rubble of Jerusalem, so we turn our thoughts to his story now.

It was almost lunchtime in the ancient Persian palace at Susa. The great hall would rival the splendor of any great hall in the palace of any great empire in any great age. Giant pillars of marble framed the vast space, draped with luxuriously colorful curtains wrapped in cords of purple and held by rings of silver. The floor was a mosaic of white, black, red, and blue stone inlay. Off in one alcove the court musicians played their instruments, adding festive background melodies to the bustle in the hall. Hundreds of nobles and satraps were seated round the great Artaxerxes, whose lovely queen sat by his side. Servants scurried everywhere, quick to respond to any request.

One face stood out among all of the servants and nobles in contrast. One face among all the festal faces was downcast in unbearable sadness. That face belonged to Nehemiah, cupbearer to the King. Nehemiah, a descendant of the Jewish slaves who had been captured years earlier in the conquest of Jerusalem, had risen to the role of servant in the palace. Born into slavery as the son of exiled Jews, Nehemiah was selected as cupbearer to the king because of diligent labor and steady trustworthiness.

"Nehemiah," The king's voice rose above the noise of the crowd. "Why does your face look so sad when you are not ill? This can be nothing but sadness of heart" (Neh 2:2).

Nehemiah was frightened to hear his name rise up like that in the presence of the guests. Yet years of training came to his aid to speak the right words. "May the king live forever!" (Neh 2:3)

He regained his composure and told his story. A few days ago his brother returned from a long trip to Jerusalem. The report was not good. With the gates burned down and the walls still in ruins, the people who lived there suffered from violence and plunder.

Everyone was surprised by the King's next response. The king asked, "What is it you want?" (Neh 2:4)

Nehemiah said a quick prayer under his breath and gulped back the fear, for the king held the power to execute him instantly for so much as a sideways look. Then he said, "If it pleases the king and if your servant has favor in his sight, let him send me to the city in Judah where my ancestors are buried so that I can rebuild it" (Neh 2:5).

After a few words back and forth about the details, the king surprisingly granted Nehemiah permission to travel all of the way from Persia to Jerusalem with permission to rebuild the walls and refortify the city.

Most of pastoral work is open-ended, without any clear physical evidence of our labor. We enter the lives of a group of people at a certain point in their journey, and we address what we can see of what they need. We vaguely hope that our influence is for the better. In contrast, transitional pastoral leadership involves a specified job for a particular time and with a visible end goal.

The book of Nehemiah is one of the greatest case studies we have on situational leadership. Consider how Nehemiah's leadership challenge has some important elements in common with the challenges given to transitional pastors. He was sent to address a lack of local leadership. He came from outside with the challenge of rallying people already on site to address their own problems.

When the initial report came about the state of Jerusalem Nehemiah had never even been within a thousand miles of those broken down walls. He already had a job—a very good job for a slave—so he certainly was not free to follow every desire. At the moment when the desire to rebuild the walls crystallized into a vision, he had neither materials nor laborers to accomplish the task. And the very idea of a rebuilt Jerusalem was abhorrent to the minor governors of all of the precincts surrounding Jerusalem. They were willing to go to great lengths, up to and including assassination, to keep Jerusalem vulnerable so that they could continue to exploit its people.

A visionary leader is not merely someone with a good imagination. A visionary leader is someone who sees a blank space—a place where the goodness of God is not abundant—and who can discern God's preferred alternative in place of what is missing. This may be physical, as in Nehemiah's vision to build the walls of Jerusalem. Or it may be relational as a transitional leader envisions a community thriving under new leadership.

Nehemiah managed to get himself appointed to rebuild Jerusalem for the sake of those who were suffering from a severe lack of leadership. Nehemiah initiated this assignment by his own choice but with the support of the established authority. He went to rebuild Jerusalem out of the compassion in his own heart for the people there, and out of the deep desire for the glory of God to be known.

A transitional leader must first rest on the promise from above and then on the passion from within. Only then will the challenge ahead make sense.

Nothing seems more impossible than how Nehemiah's dream would have appeared to him the moment before he spoke up in response to the question of the king. The barriers to fulfillment were great. But this dream became a reality. Jerusalem was rebuilt and the Jewish nation remained a cohesive collection of people, distinguishable in the world to this day.

By his willingness to speak up when asked about the inner condition of his heart, Nehemiah was given the opportunity to lead a transformational movement. Nehemiah saw the great need and his passions erupted into a quest for the restoration of Jerusalem. The passions inside of you are part of the outflow of God's promise to rescue people from the trouble they find themselves in. Your calling to shepherd a congregation through a transition may not seem as momentous as the restoration of Jerusalem following the Babylonian exile. But you will accomplish this work if you can remember every day that God cares, and you care.

Situational leadership requires professional discipline. As a specialized professional assigned to a specific type of leadership challenge the transitional pastor is constrained by three forms of discipline implicit in the story of Nehemiah. These disciplines include attention to a tyrannical timetable, a need for exceptional impulse control, and a disciplined plan for sharing information.

Tyrannical timetable Transitional pastors usually do not have an actually specified time of service. Everyone generally understands events will unfold in the search for a new pastor such that the transitional job will last anywhere from eight months to three years, depending on the unforeseeable nature of a pastoral search.[1] Implicit within this arrangement lies a tension between settling in to provide excellent pastoral leadership, and a nearly restless and fully relentless push to get the tasks accomplished so that the congregation can move forward. The question, *how long will you be here?* arises at every turn. Without projecting impatience, the transitional pastor must continually push forward with the various projects of preparing for a new leader to enter the pastoral role. Without projecting delay, the transitional pastor must encourage unhurried yet progressive reflection on the spiritual state of the congregation.

Impulse control Many and various needs must have constantly reached out to grab Nehemiah's attention. He was, after all, the kind of man who gave up a high and comfortable position in a palace in Persia for the sake of coming to the aid of a city he had never seen before in his life. His palace training most likely made him meticulously observant and also accustomed to having resources to solve any problem.

---

1. In some situations the time between pastors is brief. This puts more of a burden for transitional leadership on the new pastor. In those cases the new pastor is a kind of transitional leader. Some of our reflection here will help those pastors as they begin their ministry with the congregation still in the emotional space of transition.

The inhabitants of Jerusalem were suffering in many different ways. But their primary physical need was security, so the first job was to rebuild the walls. More than any average construction project, this job inherently created a multitude of ways to get distracted and diverted. Nehemiah's vocation, his calling to rebuild those walls meant maintaining a resolute focus on that one primary task until it was complete. Even within the completion of that one single task temptations abounded to act before thinking or to rush into ill-advised decisions. Situational leadership requires constant meditation on the main plan and the reasons for that plan, which results in a natural flow of work towards the main goal.

Disciplined plan for sharing information   Nehemiah's strategic brilliance leaps off of the page. He didn't parade into Judea with his detachment of soldiers and boldly announce that he was about to completely alter the balance of power in the region. Instead he kept a low profile for three days. He then made a confidential nighttime survey of the extent of the collapse of the walls of the city (Neh 2:11–16). The narration stresses how he kept his plans completely to himself while he undertook his own assessment of the state of things. Once the nature of the problem was firmly framed within his mind he called a meeting and announced the plan to rebuild the walls of the city clearly (Neh 2:17–18). This announcement became the starting point for rallying the energies of the people of the city who were asked to rebuild sections of the wall with their own hands. Yet this announcement also sounded the alarm for all of those who opposed the plan.

Congregations that have just lost a pastor are generally not in a position to be good at listening. They are not in a good emotional space for embracing a new leader. And they have little energy to invest in launching a new era of the life of their church. The people who normally lead initiatives in the congregation are often burned out at this point from the emotional drain of saying goodbye to the previous pastor or from all of the scrambling necessary to keep things going through the short period of leadership vacuum they have just experienced.

And yet, a comprehensive and relentless plan to communicate what is known of the plan of transition in a multitude of different ways is necessary from the beginning. In the two churches I have served as a transitional pastor I consciously used every means of communication at my disposal to clearly describe everything known about the dynamics of the transition. I wrote articles for the monthly newsletters, made references to some of the dynamics of the transition in sermons, described the nature of the transition to key leaders, and spoke about transition plans at several different smaller gatherings within the churches. I intentionally communicated more frequently than seemed necessary. And still I would say in retrospect that communications were not thorough enough.

Communicate clearly and often, then communicate some more. The information given in those communications must be strategically restrained. People will be listening with their emotional ears, not their informational ears. The details of what has been said will circulate through the congregation and will eventually come back around. You will hear what is being said and you will sometimes wonder how such a clear message could be distorted in such fascinating ways. Each round of communication must be calibrated to speak clearly within the context of the story that is emerging.

Not everyone was thrilled to discover that Nehemiah had arrived on the scene to secure Jerusalem. A trio of local leaders who had been feasting on the weakness of Jerusalem delivered their first blast of criticism but Nehemiah successfully repelled the verbal onslaught (Neh 2:19–20). At that time the governor of Samaria, just north of Judah was a man named Sanballat, who was the leader of the dissenters. Sanballat wanted to have control over the region and to be able to push the Jews around whenever it was in his interest. He didn't want Jerusalem to be secure, so he schemed to prevent Nehemiah from rebuilding. Sanballat began to throw up opposition to the rebuilding by all means available to him.

In chapter 8 of this book we will turn to Nehemiah's story again to follow the intriguing twists and turns in the drive to bring

Jerusalem back from the rubble. But before looking at those completed walls we need to consider some foundational narratives for this kind of pastoral work, beginning with a thorough look at one narrative of human loss.

5

On the Leading Edge of Loss

Psalm 137
The Story of Daniel

I was driving along a country road that winds through fields and past farmhouses on the rural edge of Portland, Oregon. The road curves a little to the left and then back to the right again. This odd little jog on an otherwise straight road is a remnant of the winding wagon trails and somewhat haphazard property boundaries of days gone by. Between those curves a bird was feeding where a tree had shed its seeds on the road. It amazes me how these birds can time their escape to avoid oncoming cars, lofting just a few feet off of the ground above the steel and glass careening their way. My windshield often comes heart-stoppingly close to fluttering feathers but they seem to always fly off quickly enough to escape by a foot or two.

As I was approaching this bird in the middle of my lane a car appeared in the other lane, coming from the opposite direction. I could see we were going to pass each other just about where that bird was. The bird fluttered to the left and stopped for a moment in the lane of that oncoming car, then fluttered back into my lane. That little bird just did not know which direction to go.

I was rooting for him, but it seemed unwise to swerve and cause a car crash over one little bird. With an oncoming car to my left and a very narrow shoulder to my right I had nowhere to go. He stood there, bewildered, in the middle of my lane, frozen with fear, hunkered down, opting not fly. My car went directly over the top of him. As soon as I was past I looked in my rearview mirror to see if he had been hit. He hadn't moved at all as my car sped over the top of him. The undercarriage of my car passed harmlessly above his head.

That little sparrow has become a symbol for me of how people feel when their world has changed. When cars can converge at fifty-five miles per hour on a sparrow out in the middle of a feast of seeds in the countryside, it seems like times have changed too much for God to keep track of all of them any more. Although that is obviously not true, when things in the world change our hearts have a difficult time still believing God is able to look after us.

And the world truly has changed. The busyness of life and the rate at which things change is more than we can handle. The trauma of a sparrow caught scratching for seeds in the nightmare of oncoming cars is only a sliver of the overwhelming levels of change faced by people every day. We hunker down and hope the threats to our well-being will pass harmlessly over our heads. We long for the way the world used to be. But that world is gone.

Every one of us has, at one time or another, gone through experiences that change our world forever. For many of our senior generation it was the experience of World War II. I have heard amazing stories of those, who, at age eighteen or twenty-three went off to war and saw things this world has never seen before. They could never go back to the innocence they knew before.

For others the world was changed by the loss of a deeply loved career. Some have been replaced by a computer or displaced by the overseas drift of labor. Others have seen their hopes of success dashed. At one time they lived with a purpose—building a small business from the ground up or working toward some fulfilling goal. Eventually they came to the point where reality closed down the dream. Dreams, in all of their infinite variety, come to fulfillment for only a precious few. For all of the rest, whatever it was is gone.

The loss of a way of life, a career, or a dream may be a somewhat small loss in comparison with those who have lost someone deeply loved. Some have lost parent, a child, a spouse, or a friend. Through death, estrangement, or the steady drift of years, people endure great upheavals in relationships.

Many of these kinds of change and loss touch the lives of the people of a congregation. And then their pastor announces he or she is leaving and the losses start to mingle in complicated ways.

How can God be God when my way of life has forever changed? How can God be God when what I love is gone?

As transitional pastors we are entrusted with the vocation of walking with people out of the land of loss into a new place filled with redemption and hope. Look with me for a moment at one of the prime biblical narratives of loss.

Life Against the Backdrop of an Irrevocable Loss

Loss is the looming factor in everything that takes place in the book of Daniel. Daniel is a person who scratched out an answer to the question, "How can God be God when what I love is gone?" When he was still a boy his country was conquered, his king was captured, his temple was pillaged, and he was taken into slavery a thousand miles away from his homeland. Yet in spite of all this loss, Daniel lived a good and full life, a life much different than his boyhood dreams could have projected. His life was an answer to that question, "How can God be God when what I love is gone?" And it was a good answer.

It was the third year of the reign of Jehoiakim when the Babylonians came and threw up a siege around Jerusalem. The king and the city fell. In get-to-the-point reporting, verse two of the first chapter of Daniel takes details fraught with tragedy and calmly tells us, "And the Lord delivered Jehoiakim king of Judah into his hand, along with some of the articles from the temple of

God. These he carried off to the temple of his god in Babylonia and put in the treasure house of his god." (Dan 1:2)

For the people of Jerusalem, their city, the Judean King, and the temple of Solomon represented tangible proof that God was God. The walls of the city, the presence of a king in David's line, and all of the activity involved in the rituals of worship were the evidence God was powerful and could take care of the nation and the people. Those "articles from the temple," removed by Nebuchadnezzar were constant reminders of God's faithfulness, love and forgiveness. This writer might as well have said, "King Nebuchadnezzar removed the heart of the people."

We have a hard time imagining the scope of this tragedy when we hear the temple in Jerusalem was plundered. We, who shun the word "sacred," who build auditoriums to house our worship rather than cathedrals, and who are mostly opposed to royalty, have a hard time caring that some of the articles of worship were taken from the temple in Jerusalem or that Judah no longer had an independent king. But for them this loss was massive.

This particular defeat of Jerusalem happened sometime around 606/5 BC. Though the event loomed large in the lives of the people of the time, it was minor in comparison with subsequent wars in 597 and then the total destruction of Jerusalem, including the temple, in 587 BC. So Daniel was not part of that later great deportation from Jerusalem to Babylon following the entire destruction of the Temple we all know so well. But he personally went through tremendous loss. In order to capture the depth of despair inherent in making this journey into slavery in Babylon, recall what one captive wrote from the same road Daniel walked but eighteen years later. Psalm 137:1–6 captures the profound feelings of sadness flowing from the loss of deportation.

> *By the rivers of Babylon we sat and wept*
> *   when we remembered Zion.*
> *There on the poplars*
> *   we hung our harps,*
> *for there our captors asked us for songs,*
> *   our tormentors demanded songs of joy;*

they said, "Sing us one of the songs of Zion!"

How can we sing the songs of the Lord
  while in a foreign land?
If I forget you, Jerusalem,
  let my right hand forget its skill.
May my tongue cling to the roof of my mouth
  if I do not remember you,
if I do not consider Jerusalem
  my highest joy.

Verses 8 and 9 of the psalm then express the anger and out-rage flowing from this sadness in one of the most vivid and raw images in all of the Scriptures.

Daughter Babylon, doomed to destruction,
  happy is the one who repays you
  according to what you have done to us.
Happy is the one who seizes your infants
  and dashes them against the rocks.

This psalm conveys the thoughts and emotions of people who are being scraped over the hard stones of outrageous loss. We do not know if Daniel would have been pleased to smash the heads of Babylonian babies. But the anonymous poet undergoing the same experience felt that way.

So Daniel knew what it is like to have your life changed for-ever and to be plunged into the chaos of rage and despair. What do you do when forces beyond your control change your life forever? Daniel responded to this tragedy in ways that forged his character to the glory of God. He could have given up on his faith. He could have said to himself, "If God can't do a better job of protecting my life then I had better find another god I can trust."

But Daniel did not come to that conclusion. Instead he held on. He stood up. The contours and textures of just how he stood up when he had been knocked down form a concrete picture of resis-tance in the context of loss. There are a number of important ways that Daniel kept the faith in a foreign land when what he loved was gone. These unfold as the emerging episodes demonstrate Daniel's resistance.

During the first series of events Daniel struggled to find ways to hold onto his integrity. He was mostly powerless against his captors. The sophisticated Babylonian culture and the impressive power of the king were meant to captivate the awe of the provincial young men. The Babylonian captors could show the boys from Jerusalem huge and stunning palaces the likes of which they had never seen. The Babylonian efficiency for administering a vast empire was on display everywhere. Vast libraries and archives of documents recorded on clay tablets demonstrated one of the most impressive writing systems ever invented. The idea was for these young men to come to appreciate everything Babylon had to offer, and, consequently, to believe their parents were bumpkins and backwater rubes. That should not have been difficult because these young men had been marched a thousand miles away from home at the age of eight to sixteen—a time when it takes very little to convince you that your parents are completely defective.

Practically speaking the king's efforts to turn these hearts from their roots to their new home involved the typical bribe. They were given a daily portion of food from the king's own table. They were invited to dine on the best food in town and offered the best wine. Down through history far greater compromises have been bought for lesser restaurant bills than this.

Now when Daniel was informed that he had been chosen to be one of those to be marched to Babylon, was this good news or bad news? Imagine the moment when the word came to young Daniel. *Our country has been conquered. For your punishment you will be sent to college on a full scholarship. You will be forced to eat at the royal steak house and drink nothing but microbrews and estate-bottled wines.* Is that good news or bad news? What would that news be to you?

Loss is always in the eye of the beholder. In spite of all the luxury, in spite of the opportunities for advancement and self-importance, this was bad news to Daniel. Leaving his homeland and being separated from the temple in Jerusalem amounted to a great loss that could never be offset by any of the rewards of Babylon.

When a pastor leaves a congregation the whole church system goes through changes perceived as loss to the system. Peter Steinke notes this when he writes, "Common to many church families is the unworked grief that surrounds the loss of an endeared pastor."[1] As we think about congregational transitions, several elements of how Steinke constructed that sentence leap off the page. This unworked grief is not simply a fading element of the first six months following the departure of a beloved pastor. Steinke is talking about church system troubles that could have an effect over decades.

I know of one congregation very well served for many years by a pastor who had hit his stride in life right at the time when he began serving this church. For fifteen years the church experienced a golden age of productive and joyful life together. When time for retirement came the pastor took various actions to help the congregation make the transition to new leadership. He prepared people for his retirement by announcing in advance that it was coming. He resolved to let the congregation move on by purposefully choosing to stay completely away for one year following his retirement. He also paid close attention to separation ethics and made a commitment not to overshadow his successor by visiting members of the congregation in the hospital or by doing weddings, funerals or baptisms without the permission of the new pastor.

For one year the retired pastor and his wife traveled extensively and found several ways to be completely gone from the community. A pastor nominating committee was formed and within that same year the new pastor had been chosen and was brought into leadership of the church.

Unfortunately the arrival of the new pastor coincided roughly with the renewed participation of the beloved retired pastor. Having been so thoroughly restrained by taking a year to be completely away, the retired pastor and his wife returned to participation in

1. Steinke, *How Your Church Family Works,* 38.

the life of the church. From their point of view this represented a vote of confidence in the new, young pastor who had been selected. A hint of the trouble ahead was between the lines of what the retired pastor's wife said to that new pastor the first Sunday when they were all present together. "We are so glad to have you in our church. I feel like you will fit in well with us."

Those were, of course, encouraging words. Yet this new pastor was clearly being measured by how he fit in with the previous pastor. As coming events revealed, the pastor's wife was not the only one taking this measurement. Everyone in the congregation was still living in the way things had been. They had lost their beloved pastor *as pastor*, but he was still in the community as their friend. They never really gave up emotionally on the way things were when he was their pastor. The passing of time softened most memories of his weaknesses and shortcomings. From an emotional standpoint, many of the people of the congregation were framing everything that happened within their inner effort to deny that any real loss had taken place.

Having received a somewhat cold reception by some of the members, the new young pastor focused on evangelism. He successfully brought in several new young families and the church facilities were strained to accommodate all of the new people. In the mind of this new pastor that reality represented a strong affirmation of his ministry. But for those still clinging to the memory of their retired pastor, this was perceived as an unwanted change. The new pastor had a better relationship with the new families than he had with those who had been part of the church for many years. Those longtime members perceived that as the new pastor's fault.

Frustrations began to boil over after the new pastor had been in place for three and a half years. None of the new members were being invited to take part in the leadership of the church. The new pastor's efforts to incorporate more of the newer members in the leadership of the church was interpreted as an effort to cast aside those who had been part of the church for a longer time. Soon this conflict circulated through the congregation and plans were made to seek the resignation of this pastor. Before another year had gone by the pastor was asked to resign.

The church soon hired an interim pastor. Little time was wasted in finding another young pastor willing to come and serve. After three years had gone by this second young pastor sensed the same resistance. By his own choice he moved on to another congregation.

So now the church engaged its third interim pastor in less than a decade.

On the surface this seemed like a congregation set in its ways and having difficulty changing with the times. A closer look reveals evidence that the difficulties centered around an unwillingness to accept the loss of the "endeared pastor," to use Steinke's phrase.

In another congregation experiencing a similar situation with a beloved pastor retiring, the new young pastor had none of these initial problems. Things went well for nine years. But then, after a protracted illness, the retired pastor died. Over the course of the next three years an odd and unexplainable bitter spirit took root in the congregation. What had been a thriving ministry turned sour and in three years things deteriorated dramatically. More than one observer felt that the grief from the death of the retired pastor brought up unresolved grief from his retirement, which led to a surprising drop in the healthy functioning of the congregation. The emotions of loss simply do not show themselves in systematic ways on the surface.

Such are the problems for congregations transitioning from quality leadership. It is unrealistic to think that another quality pastor would be able to simply step into programs and ministry functions and keep them going just the way the previous pastor did. A church family system resists the changes stemming from the loss of a pastor, and many of the individuals in the system are often doing the same. Those individual responses are no less important than the reaction going on in the whole system. As for Daniel, whose loss can only be understood when we pay attention to what it meant to him, the way each individual is experiencing the loss of their pastor can only be properly respected when we let their own point of view on the loss govern.

What about the people who are glad the pastor is gone?

When we consider the emotions arising from the loss of a pastor, most people think of the sadness from missing the skills or the particular personality of a beloved pastor. But change, even if it stems from the loss of a pastor who is considered tremendously flawed, will prove surprisingly disruptive as well. Even the person who is identified as the chief antagonist of the previous pastor will experience loss. Consider these three leaders from three different churches.

Annette might be described as more than a longtime member. In fact, her family name was scattered through the minutes of the leadership board for more than 120 years. Five generations of her ancestors preceded her in the congregation, and she felt as though that gave her greater insight than others into the truest values of the congregation. Fads of church leadership may come and go, but this congregation was regarded by Annette as a living testament to the resilience of certain principles. The pastor was a great innovator, and she found herself constantly confronted by Annette. "The church exists for those who have not yet heard Christ's message of love," was a favorite saying of this pastor. Annette cringed inside every time she heard that, but she felt proud of herself that she never openly opposed the pastor on a personal level. Instead she redoubled her efforts to volunteer for any position that might help her maintain a balance between the outreach to new people and taking care of those who had been in the church for years. Since the pastor always took the side of outreach, Annette constantly countered with considerations of the traditions that had made the church great in the past, while she lifted the priorities of the long time church families for consideration.

In another church, *Ken* was one who took pride in keeping his church financially afloat. As the church treasurer, his financial reports were always meticulous and always distributed on time. He knew several people at the bank where the church's account was held. Whenever he would stop by to make a deposit or some other transaction he would take a minute to visit with the branch manager, who was a member of another prominent church in town. These two would often enjoy a little good-natured back and forth humor about the denominational differences between their respective churches. But whenever they talked about pastors they were in agreement. Pastors do not know anything about managing finances. Ken would glance around the bank's lobby to see if anyone was in earshot. When no one was nearby he would tell stories about some of the horrendous ideas his pastor had come up with. Sometimes it was on the budgeting side of things. Sometimes it was needless expenditures on the church building. Sometimes it was naïve expectations about how much money people would be willing to give to the church. Always when Ken spoke of the pastor it was in a tone of thinly veiled derision. Now Ken's pastor has moved on to another congregation.

In still another church, *Spenser* might have been considered the unofficial chief administrator. Having spent many years running the operations of an office, Spenser understood the value of policy. He simply detested the tendency of the board to always take every decision on a case-by-case basis, so he pushed instead for the board to become chiefly the makers of policy that would then be carried out by the staff. Meetings were long and tedious because the pastor did not support the idea of turning every decision that came before them into a question of policy. Long and painful arguments would take place about the correct procedures for the elders to consider any piece of business. One time the pastor lost his temper and shouted at Spenser, "This is a church. It is not some business," in an open meeting. A lengthy series of meetings with third party mediators was necessary to patch up the fallout of that particular exchange. When the pastor announced he was leaving, Spenser was nearly giddy, but he knew he had to contain his joy because of all those around him who were in tears.

So how will the loss of a pastor affect these three? Though the surface impression might suggest that these three will not be experiencing any loss at all when the pastor leaves, it is a primary task of a transitional pastor to look beneath the surface for a counter-narrative. That does not mean theorizing about how each of these three must have liked at least something about the previous pastor. Each of these brief stories practically shouts out a narrative of a complicated loss in the absence of the "hated" pastor.

Loss is often tied to identity. When word came to Daniel that he was being shipped to Babylon, a large part of his identity had to die. Identity can be positive or it can be formed in conflict, as over against another person.

Annette could feel her own importance as the primary champion of church tradition and the loss of her protagonist might mean an end to that role.

Ken might quietly be in fear when his pastor leaves. What if the next pastor is a second career pastor, and what if her first career was as a bank manager? What would Ken be if someone like that became the next pastor? We might think any pastor with a little financial savvy would be a source of great joy to Ken. But my experiences tell me that someone like Ken feels important in his role as financial protector of the church. A financially knowledgeable pastor might upset all of that.

Spenser's role as chief keeper of the rules was only ensured with a pastor who was willing to be his opposite. Will such dynamics prevail in the future?

Transitional pastors are more effective when we step back or turn to look sideways in order to perceive a different narrative than the one presented on the surface. Without getting too deep into psychologizing about what is happening inside the people of the congregation we can simply observe that people who get themselves into a pattern of always playing the antagonist are often doing so to prevent the uncomfortable feeling of intimacy. They need constant interactions within a community. Everyone needs to belong somewhere. Yet they are uncomfortable with simple, close interactions, especially the ones that reveal the true self or that require straightforward acknowledgment of someone else. So to stay alive they participate in the emotional system of a community by negative and distancing interactions. Richardson describes this well. "One of the tricky things about closeness and distance is that most outwardly independent people are only pseudo-independent. They use distance as a way of controlling their fears about closeness. They may have tremendous needs for closeness, but have become afraid of it, so they distance instead."[2]

A transitional pastor does not need to become the psychotherapist for the entire church's emotional makeup. But it is very helpful to understand the surprising possibilities for a multitude of quirky ways that the dynamics of loss might be at work in every interaction.

When I was seventeen years old and in my senior year of high school I had a conversation with my grandmother about her experiences when she was graduating from high school. She told me, "When I graduated from high school many of the people in my graduating class were sad to be moving on, but not me. Throughout all of my high school years I took advantage of every opportunity that came my way. If there was a dance on Friday night, I went. If there was a club that interested me, I joined. If there was a sporting event I would go watch. I made the best friends and we had a great time. But by the time graduation came around I had done everything there was to do in high school. I was ready to go on. The people who were sad to graduate were the ones that never really lived their lives in high school."

Some of this wisdom may also apply to the end of a pastoral era. Those who lived in the present, who most appreciated the pastor's sermons, who were closest to the pastor, may have an uncomplicated sense of their loss. They know exactly what they will miss. They will be the most free to anticipate a new pastoral era that may be very good while being very different from the irreplaceable gifts of what has gone before.

So how do you shepherd a congregational family system and all of the individuals in it as they make their way through this complex picture of loss?

Be aware when people are treating you as though you were the previous pastor and resist falling into the pattern. Be polite, but be resolute.

2. Richardson, *Family Ties That Bind*, 20.

Be willing to walk alongside people in their grief.

Cooperate with the energy to change things, but refrain from putting your imprint on anything.

Encourage the growth of new congregational leadership.

Fully engage in the difficult tasks of bringing some things to an end from the previous era.

Though we could never even begin to try to make people face their losses as Daniel did, the narrative of his life in Babylon paints a picture of handling loss well. Even though he was not able to see his family or live in his homeland or worship at the temple of his God, he held on to those things on which he would never compromise. At the time of trial he found his voice to live according to an inner light that said, *Some things are true, and you will not force any compromise out of me.*

Daniel was not alone. His three famously named friends—Shadrach, Meshach and Abednego—shared his heroics in loss. The strength of character kneaded into their lives by resisting where they could, changed how they faced every episode of adversity that followed. We all remember the stories about the fiery furnace and the lion's den. Flannelgraph images of lions and flames are permanently fixed in my imagination from exciting Sunday school stories. But the fiery furnace and the lion's den episodes were destined to happen once Daniel and his friends found their equilibrium between their resolve to speak up in defiance and their willingness to compromise wherever possible. Once people resolve to live in freedom the rest of the heroic deeds follow as a matter of course. Though they remained slaves, these four became powerful people as they made an effort to assert their choice over against the king.

The most important change was not in the Babylonians or in their system of interacting with slaves but in the hearts of the young men who were in captivity. As they asserted their will, quietly, their lives were changed. No longer were they passive victims. They became strong by recognizing that though they could not control the events around them, they could make choices that would put them back in control of their own lives.

Passive victims are paralyzed by the circumstances of life. But whenever these four encountered a blow the response became, "Okay, what can I do about this? Where do I have power? Who can help me out? What are my options?"

Instead of letting the circumstances depress them they could get to work on the things under their control.

As Daniel held to his integrity, compromised when he could, and looked for opportunities, he grew to love the new life and the people he was forced to serve. Sincere love flows from Daniel toward the various kings of Babylon. Daniel remained true when his life was shattered. Through genuine love of people whom he never would have chosen to know he found liberation from the chains of loss.

Both of the churches I served in an interim capacity were coping with a denominational change at the same time as a pastoral change. This created a sort of complicated grief because it represented two very different kinds of loss provoking feelings of emptiness and of being cut off from important relationships of the past. In both cases the negative elements in the separation from the previous denomination engendered feelings of injustice regarding the conditions imposed for leaving the denomination. Yet the various members of the church responded with very different reactions to those conditions. In some brief tense moments conflict arose between people. Some wanted to vent their anger at how they were treated. Others wanted to forgive and forget. The varying reactions to the loss can themselves become a source of conflict.

While this kind of emotional incongruity between congregational members happens in churches throughout all stages, it is probably more likely to emerge during a transition.

Transitional pastors can be effective in leading people through loss by asking good questions. Asking people, *Why are you angry?* may help them to recognize that anger is often secondary, while sadness is primary. People who can live in their sadness for a time are able to move beyond it. Listening for the emotional words, and being secure enough to endure the twists and turns of their confused anger may help people perceive the story behind the outburst.

People going through loss often isolate themselves. So it may be helpful to ask, *Who else is going through similar feelings about this?* If you sense that several people are feeling a variety of powerful emotions it may be helpful to take time to gather them together to face what they are going through and spend group time within the reality of the pain.

It is also powerful to ask, *What resources of our faith will help us to move toward healing?* And finally, as people are ready to move into a new way of living beyond the losses they feel, the question animating all of the story of Daniel and his friends may suggest a pathway toward a new land: *Where do you have power?*

Daniel thrived when others would have merely survived by seizing opportunities. Rather than moping around and pining for the Judean hills of his youth, he looked for opportunities in this very new and very different land.

When life changes very few people look upon the changes as release from prison. We thrash about inside the rage of our own egos protesting that it is unfair for things to change. We imagine God is somehow having difficulty maintaining a grip on eternal sovereignty merely because our tiny world is being altered. The experience of losing a pastor, of thrashing around in a transition, in selecting a new pastor, and in embracing the renewed (and different) mission of the church is of the same fabric as Daniel's life of living with loss. As a transitional pastor, your job is to shepherd people towards responding to their loss with no less grace than Daniel responded to his. All of the good qualities and depth of character earned in the crucible of transition are meant to prepare people for the work ahead in their new life as a congregation.

6

Transitional Leadership and Transformation

Eustace Scrubb has become a dragon. From the beginning of C. S. Lewis's book, *The Voyage of the Dawn Treader*, the reader has been getting to know one of the most vivid and unique characters ever created by Lewis. When the book began Eustace was about as ornery as a dragon even though he was just a boy. As the book progresses he *literally* becomes a dragon. "Sleeping on a dragon's hoard with greedy, dragonish thoughts in his heart, he had become a dragon himself."[1]

After a series of dragon episodes, early one morning Eustace is back to his old self. He comes to the beach where the others in the travelling party are sleeping. He tells the whole story to his cousin Edmund of what happened to make him "un-dragoned." He narrates how a huge lion came to him in the moonless night. The lion led Eustace to a garden with a well in the middle of it. Eustace tried several times to claw his own way out of the dragon skin but he was unsuccessful. Then the lion tore deep into the dragon skin with his claws. Though the experience was painful,

1. C. S. Lewis, *Dawn Treader*, 81.

Eustace was liberated from his huge dragon body. But the removal of the dragon skin was not the end. He continues the story, saying, "Then he caught hold of me—I didn't like that much for I was very tender underneath now that I'd no skin on—and threw me into the water. It smarted like anything but only for a moment. After that it became perfectly delicious and as soon as I started swimming and splashing I found that all the pain had gone from my arm. And then I saw why. I'd turned into a boy again . . ."[2]

Like Eustace Scrubb, congregations can become dragons. Dragons live in caves filled with treasure. They breathe fire to instantly incinerate any threat to their hoard. Full-on dragon status is not how life begins for churches. Every church has a history of rich service and wonderful encouragement. A collection of people has been gathered with visions of human community as it was meant to be. Such a community naturally gathers resources as people bring their love, their money, their time, and their talent into the storehouse of the collective community.

While we all know what it is like to be a flawed church, it is helpful to crystallize a vision for what treasures lie at the heart of a good church—the kind of church we all would long to join. As I see it, four general areas constitute the living treasure at the heart of any thriving congregation. These may look very different at different times, in varying settings, and across widely divergent cultures. These elements will vary over time in the life of any congregation. But if a church really had it all, it would have an abundance of these four things: *meaningful worship of the Living God, growing relationships in which the people of the congregation share all of life's triumphs and struggles together, effective outreach inviting new people into relationship with God through Jesus Christ, and sacrificial service to neighbors outside of the church both locally and around the world.*

Certainly others would express this differently than I do. Some might add things to this list. I have heard long debates about how items three and four relate to one another—whether one is more important than the other, or whether one naturally flows out

2. Ibid., 96.

of the other, or whether evangelism and service should be entirely separated from each other. Those are all very important theological and strategic questions. But for now I point to these four things as the basic inventory of the treasures stored in the heart of an effective church. When someone has experienced even a moment of meaningful worship of God within the gathering of a particular church the memory of that moment is a pearl without price. When people find friends in a church who will love them unconditionally they will defend the treasure of those friendships at all costs. If people sense that their church is a place where hopeless and lost people could find a relationship with God that would transform their lives then they will recognize their congregation as worthy of tremendous support. And if they sense that their church makes a difference to the well-being of the community, if they feel the world in general would suffer in some way if their church was suddenly absent from the scene, they will value their church. It will feel like a tremendously rewarding thing to belong to a group that unquestionably makes a difference in the quality of life on this planet.

Most churches are places where these four gifts have been freely shared and mutually treasured from time to time. Sometimes people have experienced all four of these things in abundance in their church. For other churches these are only glimpsed now and then. And if things have not gone well in the recent past then maybe these four treasures represent nothing more than a vision of what could be. Still, whether as vision or memory, these four treasures may be seen as a brilliantly shimmering jewels stored at the heart of the community. But stored treasure is always a temptation for hoarding. The hoard becomes a danger if the congregation sleeps on the hoard—that is, rests itself on the treasure rather than resting their faith in the God who gave them the treasure in the first place. Grasping ruins these treasures. The more people reach to protect their own way of worshipping the less meaningful it is. The same is true of the other three treasures.

Individuals in churches develop a sense of great need for how the community feeds their lives. The vulnerability inherent in giving one's heart to the shining vision, the unseen riches of the congregation, leads to a lurking sense of protectiveness. Lewis has found a way to point the imagination towards an absolute and universal law of human nature. To sleep on a hoard of treasure with greedy thoughts eventually turns a person into a dragon. Individuals who come to rest themselves on the treasure of the church as a collection of things in the cave of the congregation's secure hold, and who protect the treasure with a sense of ownership rather than stewardship, become spiritually encased in dragonish skin. They cannot claw their way out.

Most members of a congregation think of an interim pastor as someone who fills in until the new pastor arrives. On the surface this inherent impatience may be justified as a desire to move forward once again into a productive time when the treasures of the church are being offered freely to the surrounding for the sake of extending the grace of Christ to the glory of God. But often all kinds of signs point to a more selfish and dragonish tendency to protect the hoard of treasure. To the extent that the congregation is protecting the hoard they will want to keep the transitional leader at a distance so that the dragon skin will not be visible.

Notice some of the tricky dynamics inherent in this situation. As protectors of the hoard, they will not want to acknowledge that anything is wrong with guarding the treasure. Any attempts to point out the problem will elicit a burst of flame from the snout of the dragon.

So what is a leader to do? When considering dragons it is important to accept the real limits to what natural wisdom can accomplish. Eustace cannot un-dragon himself. If a congregation is going be more than a merely helpful human organization undergoing the regular life cycle of ups and downs, if a congregation is going to be a miraculous sign of God's transcendent power unleashed in the world, then it will have to undergo a spiritual transformation.

All kinds of spiritual transformations happen in the normal course of a church's life under the leadership of a pastor. Yet some important kinds of spiritual transformation can only happen in the blank spaces of life. The space between the regular arrangements for pastoral relationships overflows with opportunities for certain types of community transformation. Excellent transitional leaders understand the unique calling to serve the spiritual growth of individuals and communities by attending to the possibilities of transformation in the uncomfortable interim.

Pastors often speak of transformational leadership. Transformational leadership appeals to the deepest motivations in the hearts of many pastors. The idea of transformation as the result of careful labor is probably the most compelling of all pastoral motivations.

And yet, not very many pastors feel they are succeeding in the goal of transformation. Most pastors wish to be transformational, but they are more often discouraged because they cannot point to transformation as the common outcome of their pastoral work. Why is that? And more importantly, how can a transitional pastor help give birth to congregational transformation?

The answers to those questions begin with taking a fresh look at the idea of spiritual transformation in the Scriptures. The Bible has a great deal to say about conversion, repentance, change, and transformation, yet I have searched in vain to find one word in either Greek or Hebrew that would gather together the various pieces of transformation under one umbrella. Instead the Bible contains a patchwork of images and words that point beyond transformation to a more complex and wordless reality.

One of the first great images of transformation in the Bible is the journey. Abraham is sent to a new land. Jacob must leave his home. Joseph goes to Egypt in chains. It is not a mere artifact of the stories that people grow into something new in the process of travelling to a new land. Consider Abraham and Sarah, called by God to walk along a road of transition, change and upheaval. God moved them from their homeland to a new land of promise. All the while God was calling them into a relationship with himself that put them at odds with the religion surrounding them. It must have been a lonely road. Somehow Abraham just could not have grown on his spiritual journey without going on a physical journey. The story of transformation is carried on the plot of the journey to a new land.

Transformation is also conveyed in the word "repentance" or "turning." All of the elements of repentance coalesce vividly in Joel 2:12–13.

> "Even now," declares the Lord,
>   "return to me with all your heart,
>   with fasting and weeping and mourning."
>
> Rend your heart
>   and not your garments.
> Return to the Lord your God,
>   for he is gracious and compassionate,
> slow to anger and abounding in love,
>   and he relents from sending calamity.

James R. Edwards points to a full understanding of the concept of repentance in the gospels.

> "Repentance" (Gk. *metanoia*) is a compound word meaning "to change one's mind" or "to alter one's understanding," thus connoting rational decision and willful act as opposed to emotive feeling. But the Greek etymology of the word needs to be augmented by the concept of repentance and conversion in the OT, particularly in the prophets, if John's call to repentance is to be appreciated. Repentance was the message of the Baptizer reduced to a word. It entailed, according to Mark's brief report in v. 4, a turning away from sin, and also, according to Matt 3:8 and Luke 3:8, a sign or "fruit," perhaps water baptism but more likely moral transformation.[3]

We tend to associate the word repentance with a spiritual state of humility and sorrow. Repentance implies simple change of direction, as the Old Testament writers often simply speak of turning or returning when they call for repentance. When considering how much damage a journey in the wrong direction can bring, humility and sorrow are the right responses. The word "turn" is

---

3. Edwards, *The Gospel According To Mark*, 31.

almost always physical, but when this means turning life completely around the movement of the body is laden with a much more profound meaning.

The English word "conform" sometimes carries negative associations, but the Greek equivalent has no such baggage. We might think of being conformed to the image of Christ as being restored to our original shape. From this standpoint it is good news to be conformed to the right image. We are creatures of a greater being than ourselves, and thus it becomes imperative to get the shape right and be conformed to that shape. With this background in mind Rom 12:2 may be the prime text of transformation. "Do not conform to the pattern of this world, but be transformed by the renewing of your mind."

That brings us to the nearest equivalent in Bible languages to our English "transform." It is surprising how infrequently the word is used given that the concept seems so central to spiritual life.

In fact, Jesus never used the word "transform" in the accounts handed down to us. Jesus relies mostly on the previously mentioned images of journey, the very descriptive word "repent" or turn around, several stories that vividly describe the process of transformation, and the image of new life or new birth, "be born again."

All of these diverse ways the Bible writers talk about transformation should alert us to how central the concept is but also how diverse the experiences of transformation can be. Though he never uses the word, Jesus's teaching is all about transformation. He never seems to speak without pointing to some element of change.

Every change has a vector, a mode, and a degree of change, and we do well to attend to the subtle mix of change elements. Conversely, to misrepresent the vector, the mode or the degree of change leads to malformation, not transformation.

So for example, Jesus says, "You are the light of the earth. A city set on a hill cannot be hidden. Neither do men light a lamp and place it under a bushel. No, but they place it on a lampstand and it gives light to all the house. Therefore, let your light shine before men that they may see your good works and glorify your Father who is in heaven." (Matt 5:14–16)

Pay attention to the transformation dynamics of this passage. Jesus does not say, "Become light. Be transformed into light." He says, "You are light." But something prevents the light from shining. The vector of transformation is to move out from under whatever hides the light. Identify what is blocking the light and get out from under whatever it is. Stay the same, but move to a place where you can be seen. The mode of transformation is the repentance mode. Understand you are not where you need to be and move. And the level of transformation in this case is not deep and inward, but outward. At other times Jesus points directly to deep and inward transformation as in Matthew 23:25–26 when he warns the teachers of the Law and Pharisees to clean the inside of the cup.

Spiritual leadership is the art and practice of directing a community to attend carefully to all of the elements of transformation within their experience in light of God's promise to lead us. This is why a narrative understanding of transitional leadership is so important. Narrative involves the movement of characters from the place where they began, through events that shape the trajectory of their movement, until they arrive at a conclusive destination. God is writing a story in the events of a congregation as they cope with whatever upheaval is taking place. Transitional leadership means attending to that narrative and participating at crucial moments in the decisive movements that will cause the community to arrive safely in their new land.

Yet the promise of arriving safely at the end of this journey in no way implies that the travel will be pain free. It is painful to a congregation to have parts stripped away. It is painful to leave behind what must be left behind. Some things must be stripped away in order to find the core identity of the congregation. This is where C.S. Lewis's metaphor of the dragon skin is so helpful in describing what we see congregations experience during a pastoral transition. Eustace does not want to be a dragon. In fact he uses the very dragonish claws he has grown to try to rip away the dragon part. But he cannot get rid of the dragon skin on his own. In his biography of Lewis, Alan Jacobs captures the significance of this part of the story.

> It is especially noteworthy that Eustace's own attempts to remove his scaly skin are ineffectual. To peel off his skin is "a most lovely feeling," but he is just the same after doing so—just as Lewis himself had been exactly the same after "breaking the neck" of a prideful thought, or several prideful thoughts. Eustace skins himself three times before realizing that his best efforts are inadequate. It is only Aslan who has the strength (and the love) to do the job properly—that is, to turn Eustace back into a boy again—and Eustace welcomes the gift, even if "the very first tear he made was so deep that I thought it had gone right into my heart."[4]

Once the dragon skin is gone a bath is necessary to seal the transformational process. Finally Eustace is dressed in new clothes. Likewise the congregation is forced to undergo a kind of tearing away of itself in the interim between pastors. Sometimes the people will claw at each other in an effort to move toward the desired end. That tearing brings pain, but no healing. Yet as the congregation makes its way from one place to another, as time goes by, God does strip away the old and does bring healing. The bath comes by God's Spirit and the new clothes are provided.

But we may not always see these things that sometimes happen over time and in secret. Transformation is not always visible, undeniable, or obvious.

So what can we do? What is the transitional leader's part in bringing transformation to a congregation in transition? As for all pastoral leadership, the first requirement is faith. Circumstances may severely challenge your ability to keep believing that what is taking place is for the salvation of the people and the glory of God. Within my years of serving congregations in transition I experienced countless times when I looked into the eyes of people who were severely shaken by painful events in their congregations. We went through budget cuts and painful downsizing of staff.

4. Jacobs, *The Narnian*, 134.

We saw staff members who had seemed like mature people display alarmingly childish and selfish behavior. We saw people who had been dear friends lash out in shocking ways. These and many more alarming experiences pushed the people of these churches toward the edge of giving up. Their sense of the real nature of the church was dismantled. Even their sense of God's presence in their lives through some of these dark events was severely challenged. The transitional pastor's vocation means being the one who still believes. This can never be a matter of sunny optimism. Cheerful platitudes will chase away the honest reflection necessary for growth. Yet within the honest acknowledgment of the difficulties, the transitional pastor is, by vocation, by assignment, out of the essence of the role, the person in the situation who resolutely believes that God is bringing the congregation to a new land of hope.

Within the strength of that faith, the transitional pastor sees the various biblical images of transformation as guides in the dark moments, new pathways in the dead ends, and opportunities for a turnaround story when someone is moving in the wrong direction.

When Someone Must Move on from His or Her Position

The most painful moments of my time as a transitional pastor have come when individuals needed to be removed from their roles in the congregation. Whether it is paid staff or volunteer leaders, the period of transition is a time when the problem of people who are a bad fit for the role they occupy becomes acute. Not having the credibility that comes from years of investing in the congregation, nor the authority that comes through holding a particular vision for the future, the transitional pastor lives with the responsibility of making the way clear for the next pastor to come in to a place where the "bad fit" leaders have been removed.

This is always difficult because "bad fit" leaders often have reasons why they are clinging to their roles. Consider Jason, who had been the youth director at his congregation for a little over a year when the pastor left. This was Jason's first full-time position out of college and he was very excited about the job when he took it. Having had lots of volunteer experience in working with youth but no actual employment on his resumé when he took the job, it was agreed that this was to be a job where he would grow in his abilities under the constant supervision of the pastor. But the last six months of the pastor's time at the church were full of conflict, and Jason had never really grown into his potential. Now the congregation was experiencing a budget shortfall and an absence of youth. Perhaps a thriving youth ministry lies in the congregation's future. Maybe Jason will go on to great things. But right now he is a bad fit for where things are with this congregation.

This is, of course, a very delicate reality in Jason's life and in this congregation. His sense of himself as a person is deeply tied to this risk he took by taking a job in a church as his very first employment out of college. And the congregation is deeply invested in his success, as they took a risk on him and they can see that most of the reason why he is a bad fit is due to the changes they have gone through and not due to his shortcomings as a leader. The few students who are still in the congregation have bonded more closely with Jason since they have lost their pastor. No one wants this to be the reality. But reality is an obdurate thing. Jason needs to move on.

The congregation may want the transitional pastor to make a unilateral decision to let the youth director go. Then everyone will be able to escape the pain of what this decision means. But this pain is itself part of the necessary growth for the congregation. If letting Jason go is too painful for the congregation then they will rally to find an alternative. Pain has a way of sorting out what we value most. Pain motivates us to action along the lines of our deepest values.

So a unilateral decision made by the transitional pastor is not best. The congregation needs patient leadership. Yet even if a perfectly just process is followed to properly work toward a fair termination, Jason's departure will cause a stir. Blaming will go on. People who know very little about the reasons for the decision will offer confident critiques of it. From beginning to end the transitional pastor simply needs to show up and faithfully walk with everyone concerned. Things will not necessarily turn out well. But leadership means making the hard decisions in the right way and then hanging with people as they feel the pain.

In countless other ways painful necessities hit congregations hard while they are in transition. A transitional pastor embraces the vocation of walking with people through these painful necessities. These unwanted and painful episodes may be the very things that God is using to bring about transformation in the congregation. But within the short time frame of a pastoral interim, the pain may remain apparent while the transformation waits to be revealed in the future.

This brings several questions to the surface. Where is the hope? What is the reality? How can a leader realistically hold onto hope through the discouraging times, and point people towards that hope when they are teetering on the edge of despair? For answers to these questions we turn to events in the life of the prophet Jeremiah.

7

Where is the Hope? What is the Reality?

Jeremiah 37, 38

Come for a moment and stand atop the walls of Jerusalem on a clear January night. David's citadel is to our right. Every star is distinct in the sky. Two figures are present on the wall. Zedekiah is the Judean King and Ebed-melech is the king's slave, a captive from the land of Cush. The two are pacing the top of the walls looking for signs that the Babylonian army is approaching to lay siege. They stare over the dark, distant land, straining to see the signal fires of Azekah. Those signal fires will be the first message indicating the Babylonian army has arrived and has begun to lay siege to the cities of Judah.

Zedekiah wrings his hands in fear that the Babylonian army is on its way. Zedekiah is a selfish and cowardly leader—not extremely evil, just incompetent and pitiable. He wants for things to turn out well but is unwilling to take any bold steps to make peace. He knows that his own weakness will be his destruction but he is paralyzed within his fears.

Right now Zedekiah is fearfully running through his options. He could surrender, but then the Babylonians may turn him over to his enemies among the Judeans who were already taken into exile into Babylon in previous waves. He could try to outlast the siege. Not much hope in that but it would delays things. He could ask for help from Egypt. That might work, but it could backfire. If he does not make any decisions he will hopelessly entangle himself in a web of fear that will make it impossible to do anything constructive about the problem.

Zedekiah may not even be able to speak the words of his cold hard regret as he stands in the chill of the night scanning the blackness for the flash of a signal fire. The Babylonian army comes in numbers far too large to understand. They carry with them the chains of his captivity.

It is a terrible thing to live hanging on a rumor and hoping it is not true, hoping the army is not coming. But he knows they will come, as they came for all of the rest of his family.

The king's Cushite servant breaks the silence. "The night is cold. They'll stay by the coast until morning at least."

"And march to the hills by morning's light—I know," Zedekiah quickly fires back.

"There is still time," the servant says.

Zedekiah grows impatient. "Time for what? Time to sit here and waste away flesh so they don't have as much to fry when they march me through the trackless wastes? Time to tear off my own thumbs so they don't have any prize to send back to Babylon? Oh, yes, there is time—time to remember every mistake I've made that backed me into this hell-corner."

After a round moment of silence the servant continues. "Shall I send any messages?"

Zedekiah smiles at this. "Always so calm. No. No messages. I am finished sending messages."

"None to the Pharaoh?"

"He hasn't answered the last three."

"No, he hasn't."

"So what would I send?"

"You haven't given up." The Cushite servant has a way of making statements that seem more like questions.

"No, I haven't given up. I've been given up." The king pauses here in a sort of sigh. "Send the same message, but say it some other way. We need help. If he could march his army north, that might provide enough diversion. We would be so grateful and so on. You write it your way this time."

"I'll bring you a translation by morning light."

"Don't bother showing me your translation. Just send it. I am through caring."

The servant bows and leaves. Zedekiah continues to peer out into the night, wondering when the signal fires will appear.

Some people walk into the story of the Bible for a moment, play a role briefly, and then quickly exit without us ever learning much about them. Such is the story with this one minor character in the book of Jeremiah, the other person on the wall with the king. Ebed-melech was a Cushite servant of Judean royal court. It is likely that "Ebed-melech" is not really his name—that we know him only by his title, since "Ebed-melech" means "servant of the king." That he comes from Cush means he is an African by birth. Most likely he was captured and made a slave. But he is a slave with some power.

Cush is often identified with Ethiopia but that designation is misleading. Cush was a much larger territory than present-day Ethiopia. It included what are now Ethiopia, Sudan and Somalia. This is a huge territory encompassing all of Northeast Africa with the exception of Egypt. Since Sudanese men tend to be tall I picture Ebed-melech towering over his Judean captors, but we know very little of this man.

At the opening of chapter 38 Jeremiah spoke plainly God's word of destruction for the city of Jerusalem, but rescue for those who would give themselves over into the mercy of the Babylonian army. A handful of officials heard Jeremiah's prophecy of destruction and they reported him to king Zedekiah. They charged Jeremiah with discouraging the soldiers by presenting this negative view.

Those who complained about Jeremiah didn't believe in evaluating Jeremiah's message by a standard of truth. They wanted to silence him based on whether or not his message inspired people to fight on the side of the king.

Zedekiah didn't agree with what the handful of accusers had said about Jeremiah. He simply let them know he would not oppose them. So Jeremiah fell into the hands of those who didn't like his message. They didn't have the nerve to kill Jeremiah directly. Instead they did to him what their ancestors did to Joseph: they threw him into a pit. This particular pit was an empty water storage cistern. No water was left. Jeremiah sank down into the mud. That mud symbolizes the hopelessness of the times. From later episodes it is clear that Jeremiah's mood was in just as muddy of a pit as this cistern. In Jeremiah's hungry and weakened state, leaving him in that cistern could be the equivalent of executing him.

Ebed-melech had most likely seen his share of battles, which made him knowledgeable of the fate awaiting anyone caught on the wrong side of power. So he had much to fear. Yet he recognized the truth of what Jeremiah had proclaimed. He found the king and lodged his objection to how Jeremiah was treated. Though he was only a servant of the king, he was able to reverse the decision that threw Jeremiah into the cistern. The very same king who could do nothing to stop the evil men from casting Jeremiah into the cistern now gave orders for Jeremiah to be rescued from the cistern.

Armed with the consent of the king, Ebed-melech hurried to the mouth of the cistern and quickly found soft cloth to wrap around the ropes to be used in the rescue. Remember, no one had eaten much in several months. Very little flesh was left to cushion Jeremiah's ribs. Any rope used to lift him out of the cistern would be painful. Ebed-melech's thoughtfulness would soften some of the pain of the rescue. The narrative takes great care to describe the compassion and thoughtfulness of Ebed-melech. Those soft cloths wrapped around the ropes of Jeremiah's rescue are an essential part of the story.

This part of the book of Jeremiah reflects a tension between hope and reality, and between truth and comfort. Genuine hope is a blanket that covers the cold truth and cushions harsh realities. Congregations in transition teeter between the unquenchable hope that comes from faith and the fearful specter of an uncertain future. Transitional leaders may be tempted to create false hope as a shield. Conversely it is also tempting to let empathy become a magnet for the despair that some in the congregation may be feeling.

Jeremiah's life is itself part of the message of his book. He lived out the struggle of his relationship with God in plain view so that the real story of faith could be made visible for the people.[1] Two forces stand out in Jeremiah's personality: his need for people and his rigid allegiance to truth. Living as he does in this era, these two needs are entirely opposed to one another. I have a difficult time comprehending how one person could exist with these two forces at war inside. Jeremiah's greatness partly lies in his willingness to suffer with the clash of these two needs.

All Alone

Starving to death and mired in the mud of a dark cistern, Jeremiah certainly represents too gloomy of an image for the life of a transitional pastor. But if we can see that dark pit as an emotional picture of the most difficult moments the Jeremiah narrative becomes a great companion story. Jeremiah was isolated from all of the people because he was called to live within both the hope and the reality of what God was doing, at a time when no one else was capable of abiding in that tension. No one else was able to see the present and live in hope, nor could they see the present and accept the reality of their situation. Often hope and reality are misconstrued as a binary choice pitting a sunny and optimistic disposition against a more honest and objective assessment of the way things are. Jeremiah's life exposed this binary view as an inadequate way of viewing events. While God was sustaining Jeremiah at every moment, the people were too fearful to face reality, and too filled with self-loathing to live in hope.

---

1. Hayner, "Suffering and the Prophetic Vocation," 457–459.

Jerusalem stood between two armies, the Babylonian and the Egyptian. So the people were caught between large and unmoving forces. No one could simply walk away. But the people in our churches can leave.

Nothing in my past prepared me to expect the resignations and departures that came like a steady drumbeat in my first interim ministry. I believed that everyone in the congregation would see how essential it was to stay with their church in a time of transition. I came to my first interim call having served three churches over the course of eighteen years. Annie and I began with an adventure, serving a beautiful native Alaskan community. We then served six years as co-associate pastors in one church, and then I served twelve years as head of staff of another church. So I was used to the way the life of a church draws new people into the fellowship. Vibrant worship and the relationships between the people of the congregation as they share life together and work to serve their communities always seemed to be the attraction that led to numerical growth in membership. I was never really convinced my preaching and my leadership were the reasons for success. Even in my highest moments of self-satisfaction with my work I always saw the addition of new members as people making a commitment to the church and not to me.

And so I never expected any members to leave when I began serving as the interim pastor of another congregation. I expected anyone who had great love and appreciation for the former pastor's ministry to stay through the interim, understanding how much life he had poured into the congregation and understanding how much it would mean to that former pastor to know that even as he left his flock behind they were still thriving. I expected those who had personally benefitted from the ministry of the congregation would see loyalty in the transition as the best way to return thanks to God for all they had been given. I thought staff members and lay leaders would see the transition time as a test of their ability to carry through on commitments they had made.

And then some resignations and departures commenced even before I had a chance to unpack all of my books.

An interim between pastors is a time when people feel free to leave. Staff members will resign or will start neglecting their core responsibilities to the point of needing to be let go. Volunteer ministry leaders will see this as a time to resign from the area in which they have been serving. Some members will start going to another church. So being an interim pastor involves having the self-control to not feel totally abandoned. No one will ever completely understand how hard your job is under these circumstances. You may have a restless congregation that desperately wants new programs and new vision to reassure them that the church is still alive and worth their time and energy. But you will spend an inordinate amount of time recruiting replacements for those who have resigned or left. And you will be doing all of this recruiting at a disadvantage. As a new leader to the congregation you will not know the gifts and strengths of people, you will not know who is a trained and trustworthy leader, and you will not have much personal persuasiveness when it comes to recruiting. You will be recruiting people to fill roles you do not completely understand yourself for a future you cannot fully articulate.

The crowd of nobles conspired to put Jeremiah into a pit. One person rescued him out of that pit. The high ranking officials were from among Jeremiah's people and they rejected him. A slave and an ethnic foreigner rescued him. Ebed-melech saw the situation clearly while the crowd of nobles could not see. At great risk Ebed-melech acted, but the leaders of Jerusalem had nothing to lose by tossing him into the pit. The soft cloths, wrapped around the rescue line represented a great deal to Jeremiah. I wonder if those cloths took on great significance for Jeremiah as a representation of God's ability to keep a promise by means of the least likely person. Jeremiah lived to record all of this because one unlikely person listened to what God was asking and took the risk to act on what he heard.

All of this is challenging. Yet like Jeremiah, whose loneliness was the necessary consequence of clinging to hope and reality at the same time, the moments of isolation of a transitional pastor may be a necessary part of the calling. If that is even partially true then something else is emphatically true. It is imperative for a transitional leader to be fully equipped to fight discouragement, to cling to hope, to believe some servant of the king is listening. So turn back with me again to a primary story of effective situational leadership and the narrative describing how Nehemiah engaged in his epic battle with discouragement.

8

The Battle against Discouragement

Nehemiah chapters 2–6

Pastors are sometimes subjected to highly discouraging events. Consider these three episodes from three separate churches.

Accidental Eaves Drop

One interim pastor tells the story of a time when he was alone in the church building around six in the evening, a time when the building was usually empty. He overheard a fairly heated discussion in the fellowship hall so he headed that way to explore what was happening. As he approached the room out of sight he could hear two of the elders in a heated argument, with voices raised to the point of nearly a yelling match. He stopped, thinking it might be unfair to "catch" these two misbehaving when they thought they were alone in the building. So he turned around and started to walk away. One sentence rang out in the air as he walked the other direction back toward his office. " . . . don't make excuses, we're a hen house with no rooster."

This was not intentional eaves dropping, because the transitional pastor never intended to hear anything, just help with a conflict situation. But some things cannot be unheard. Did that fragment of a sentence mean what he thought it meant? Was the church in this interim the henhouse, and was he the non-rooster? Or was it completely unrelated to him? The only thing to do was to let it go. But the possibility that everyone was ridiculing his leadership behind his back was a powerfully discouraging shadow.

Overzealous Treasurer

The mother of two high school students was opposed to sending them on a mission trip being planned by the youth group. Instead of simply keeping them home from the trip, she became obsessed with preventing the entire youth group from going on the trip. She expressed her opposition by sending information to other parents of students suggesting that the location of the mission trip was dangerous. The other parents were not swayed. So she attacked the integrity of the youth director, creating a false impression of immaturity. The transitional pastor did not agree. He brought the concerns before the youth committee who listened carefully to what this mother had to say. After the youth committee heard the complaint they also did not agree with the concerned mother and they expressed their support in the youth director. Wanting also to support the youth director, the transitional pastor gave his endorsement to the conclusions of the youth committee. Undeterred, the mother began to seek positions of authority in the church. She was elected to the board of elders and became the church treasurer, where she continued to express her opposition.

The next attack came indirectly. The church had set up a medical reimbursement agreement as part of the compensation of the transitional pastor. The disgruntled mother-turned-treasurer refused to allow a medical bill of the transitional pastor's to be reimbursed, questioning the validity of the bill. She did this even though all procedures that were set up for reimbursement had been followed. Since the transitional pastor had already paid the bill and was only seeking reimbursement, the delay in reimbursement represented a frightening strain on the finances of the transitional pastor's family. Even worse, the requests for additional documentation of the precise medical condition being treated sent a shock wave through the transitional pastor's family, who were craving confidentiality in the case of one particular illness. The youth group did go on their trip and found it to be one of the most life changing events for many of them. But the transitional pastor was left feeling wounded and vulnerable.

Directing More than the Choir

Another transitional pastor was surprised when a wave of people from the congregation contacted him with great concern over the supposed firing of a longtime choir director. In truth the choir director had resigned, but some form of dissatisfaction led this person to go to various groups in the church and tell a different story about the event. Eventually the story was straightened out but the transitional pastor was left with a bad taste.

Nehemiah endured similar problems and his story should be the constant companion of transitional leaders who may face opposition. Earlier, in chapter 4, we considered the beginning of Nehemiah's story. His passion for the well-being of a city he had never seen moved him to speak to the king. Nehemiah defied all expectation by successfully being appointed to rebuild the walls of Jerusalem. Though he started out as a palace slave, by the end of the book of Nehemiah Jerusalem was transformed from a pitiful ruin to a thriving city. The journey of his life may be one of the greatest stories of prevailing in an uphill battle.

Chapter 3 of the book of Nehemiah chronicles an amazing cooperative effort in great repetitive detail. The work of rebuilding the wall of Jerusalem was an absolutely massive effort. Remarkably, the painful labor was accomplished not by slaves who had no other choice, but by the free people of Jerusalem who cooperated to make their own lives better. When a group of people takes on a challenge expressing their determination to be free, opposition often arises to quell the freedom. Sanballat the Samaritan was outraged. He rallied the opposition against the rebuilding of Jerusalem. He impulsively constructed various schemes to prevent the fortification. Sanballat represents that opposing person who will instantly present a roadblock to progress.

Nehemiah was pressed to stand up against six facets of discouragement coming his way. When various kinds of discouragement all come at once the flexibility required to deftly counter each type of discouragement is highly demanding. Let's take a look at these six types of discouragement.

Ridicule Nehemiah 4 is the story of mounting opposition to Nehemiah's leadership and vision. Knowing the end of the story—the walls were rebuilt and Jerusalem began a new life as a city—takes the entire sting out of the ridicule. From the vantage point of history, the ridiculers are ridiculous. But while Nehemiah was in the middle of the story, ridicule was a formidable weapon.

Fear Fear that corrodes hope leads to discouragement. Ezekiel 21:12 and Zephaniah 3:16 utilize a profound biblical metaphor of despondent weakness. "Slack hands" portray a picture of a people who have been overcome by fear. And that fear leads to an inability to raise the hands to accomplish anything. One way or another, fear tends to syphon off energy. When the wall had been rebuilt to half its height Nehemiah's opponents threatened to attack the workers as they engaged in their labor (Neh 4:7). Nehemiah was forced to take some of the workers out of the building project and post them as guards (Neh 4:13).

Deception In the first encounter Sanballat immediately labeled Nehemiah as "rebellious" against the king (Neh 2:19). When the repairs were halfway finished Sanballat organized a joint effort to attack and spread confusion (Neh 4:7–8). When that plan was thwarted he pretended to want to meet with Nehemiah to discuss the situation, when in fact he was secretly plotting to lure Nehemiah into an ambush (Neh 6:2). He tried that tactic four times (Neh 6:4). The fifth time he sent a letter accusing Nehemiah of organizing a revolt against the king and threatened to send a false report of the supposed revolt to the king. Finally Sanballat hired a false prophet to tell Nehemiah to flee to the temple because a band of assassins supposedly had been deployed to end Nehemiah's life (Neh 6:10–13).

All of this deceptiveness was designed to end the good work Nehemiah was doing—if not by actually eliminating Nehemiah, then at least by discouragement. Nehemiah offered a constant refrain of prayer in response to the episodes of deception. His prayer centered on his true wish that his deceptive enemies would be brought to account before God for what they had done.

False Accusations   A central component of deceptive discouragement is the strategy of throwing up as many accusations as possible and watching to see what sticks. The tense exchange between Nehemiah and his three opponents in Nehemiah 2:19–20 narrates both the typical tendency of opponents to toss out the first accusation that comes to mind and the best response to accusations. In this scene Nehemiah has taken his initial steps to assess the situation and he has laid out his vision of rebuilding the walls. Three leaders from neighboring regions heard the plan and accused Nehemiah of rebelling against the king.

This accusation flowed entirely from a desire to discredit Nehemiah publicly. It arose out of an impulse and not after careful reflection. The accusers hoped to get a stammering self-justification in response. They hoped Nehemiah would come off as defensive.

The reader of Nehemiah's book is aware that these accusations are totally false. We began listening to this story in the very palace of the king. We heard the conversation that initiated the rebuilding project. We know from verses 7–9 of chapter 2 that Nehemiah had all the authority of the throne behind him in the form of letters authorizing the work and a military detachment to back the letters. We also know (Neh 2:10) Nehemiah's accusers were completely aware that the project was entirely authorized by the king.

Nehemiah's response did not address the false accusations at all, even though he had in his possession the very letters from the king that would factually negate the accusation. If he would have pulled out the letters to show the accusers and the crowd at that moment he might have put to rest this one particular claim, but he would have opened the project to an endless string of objections. The number of false accusations is only limited by the imagination of the false accuser. If Nehemiah would have taken the time to factually dispute the accusation he would have tacitly invited the accusers to present every objection they could think of in the future. Instead Nehemiah pointed the attention of all who were listening to God as the ultimate judge of their efforts. He then reminded the accusers that they had no standing to present complaints, since the rebuilding of Jerusalem was not their concern. In reality they were meddling in the affairs of their neighbors.

Rumors of Danger   Sanballat had tried four times to lure Nehemiah into a good place for an assassination. Each time, Nehemiah resisted. So Sanballat sent a "rumor has it" message, containing all of the telltale signs marking rumors as entirely different from true expressions of concern (Nehemiah 6:6–7).

Rumors frequently begin with an overstatement of how widely the supposed information has been circulating. In this case the story is supposedly circulating "among the nations." Now it is true that the Hebrew word for "nations" does not imply the vast countries we imagine when we read that English word. "Nations" merely means "peoples" or various groups of persons of varying sizes. Still the phrasing makes the number of people who affirm the veracity of the report seem quite large. In churches we hear the phrase, "People are saying . . . " or "Everybody is talking about . . . " This overstatement of the number of people involved in the report is one of the classic signs that the rumor process is at work.

Always be wary of someone who believes a report to be more credible if more people are discussing it.

The report moved on to the second classic telltale sign of rumor—confirmation by an authority. Nehemiah was told that Geshem was also saying what "the nations" were reporting (Neh 6:6). That is the logical fallacy of aggregating non-credible sources to create the illusion of greater credibility.

The rumor then moved to a personal level. The rumor stated that all of the rebuilding efforts were designed by Nehemiah to set himself up as king of Jerusalem.

Some of the substance of the rumor was undeniable. That is how rumors work. The city *was* being rebuilt. A rebuilt Jerusalem would surely strengthen the political power of Nehemiah. Those parts were true. In addition, Nehemiah would surely have loved to see an independent kingdom restored for Judah. Whether or not he was personally ambitious to actually be the king of Judah is unknown. I cannot imagine very many people in Nehemiah's role who would not have dreamed from time to time about actually being the king of the city he was rebuilding. This rumor functioned as an upsetting assertion containing compelling elements of truth mingled in with innuendo and falsehood.

Verses 8–9 of chapter six might serve as a step-by-step guide for responding to rumors. First, Nehemiah sends back a complete statement of denial contained within the sphere of the source of the rumor. He does not publish a denial to the supposed "nations" who are purported be spending all of their time talking about the issue. He simply sends back the message to the one who sent the rumor. And he does not engage with splitting hairs about the partial truths in the rumor. His message is brief and not blunted by subtle nuances. "Nothing like what you are saying is happening, you are just making it up out of your head." (Neh 6:8)

Corruption of Friends

Nehemiah's story includes an episode that may serve as a warning. A prophet named Shemaiah urges Nehemiah to flee to the temple and lock the doors. He claims that men are on their way to kill Nehemiah. Resisting the fears raised by this prophecy, Nehemiah refused to do anything defensive in response to this word. Perhaps shaken, Nehemiah remained unmoved by the threat and he came to understand that Shemaiah was only making this claim to assist Sanballat.

This has been a long and somewhat frightening list of ways Nehemiah engaged in battle against forces of discouragement. Nehemiah never was pinned down by this array of discouraging events. The main purpose of Nehemiah's story is to narrate the activity of God in restoring Jerusalem as promised. Within that main story lies the important lesson of how God used the skills of Nehemiah to accomplish the task. Consider how this story is also a case study for many kinds of discouragement. Nehemiah makes it through his times of discouragement and he prevails over every force for discouragement, and you and I can too. Here are some ways to counteract these six kinds of discouragement.

Enduring Ridicule

I never experienced intentional ridicule throughout my two lengthy times of service to churches in transition. I suspect such treatment is rare. Yet criticism may easily swing over to the column of ridicule during an unlikely convergence of events, creating unintentional ridicule. Unintentional ridicule is likely, even inevitable when people are agitated by the changes in their world. Some transitional leaders enter a situation where the previous pastor was dismissed for misconduct. Some churches have lost a large percentage of their membership because the previous pastor created a church split and drew many members to start a new church in the very same community. These events provoke outrage in the individuals of the congregation, but few outlets exist to express those intense emotions. Some people become virtual fountains of sarcasm when they have no honest way of hitting back in response to the sucker punch of a trusted pastor running amok. That fountain of sarcasm may flow toward a transitional pastor.

Nehemiah's prayer (Neh 4:4–5) in response to ridicule represents an honest first step. "Hear us, our God, for we are despised. Turn their insults back on their own heads. Give them over as plunder in a land of captivity. Do not cover up their guilt or blot out their sins from your sight, for they have thrown insults in the face of the builders."

This prayer seems to stand in opposition with the words of Jesus. "You have heard that it was said, 'Love your neighbor and hate your enemy.' But I tell you, love your enemies and pray for those who persecute you, that you may be children of your Father in heaven. He causes his sun to rise on the evil and the good, and sends rain on the righteous and unrighteous" (Matt 5:43–45).

The prayer of Nehemiah is the honest and natural response to discouraging ridicule. We who follow the teaching of Christ tend to suppress prayers like those of Nehemiah as they rise up inside of us. *I should pray for those who are hurting me,* we lecture ourselves. This may lead to stagnation as we hover between the suppressed prayers calling for judgment and phony prayers of blessing that we honestly do not feel at all.

The stagnation may be broken by intentionally returning to the prayer of Nehemiah and honestly praying in that way concerning those who have hurt us. Go ahead. Tell the God of grace to fully punish the people who have hurt you. Linger for a time with your longing for punishment fully exposed in prayer. When prayers for vengeance are held honestly before God the result will be an inward revolution so that imprecations and calls for judgment morph into the blessings of Jesus. I have found I can never honestly sit before God and ask for his judgment to come to someone without eventually understanding how utterly lost I am if God's true judgment is given evenly to everyone. I am transformed into a person who longs for God's mercy.

Refusing to Be Discouraged by Fear

A searching inner light is necessary. Transitional leaders must be able to ask themselves, "Am I afraid?" Unacknowledged fear can lead straight to a frozen state. Indecision follows and fear has accomplished its goal. Yet recall that Nehemiah did not merely try to think his way beyond fear, nor did he simply try to pray the fear away. He did pray, but he also posted guards to protect the workers (Neh 4:9). Take the actual steps necessary to address the conditions leading to fear.

Countering Deception

Sanballat represents a type of person every transitional pastor may meet from time to time. Deception is morally acceptable to this person because some other goal is more important than maintaining truthfulness.

It may take every leadership virtue available to combat the deceptiveness. Throughout the exercise of that virtuous leadership a battle against the corrosively discouraging effect of deceptiveness is also imperative. Deceptive people are often energized when they are thwarted. The more successful you are at repelling their schemes the more they seem to gleefully move towards a different angle.

A transitional pastor must strive to maintain an inner calm in the face of discouraging deceptiveness. Nehemiah lives in the security of a rich prayer life throughout this frightening and discouraging deceptiveness. Consider what equivalent prayers you might want to lift against the deceptive people who are discouraging you.

Countering False Accusations

I know of one transitional pastor who faced a confusing array of false accusations. Just moments before the monthly meeting of the board of elders, word came that an individual member from the congregation was going to show up unannounced at the meeting to lodge a complaint.

This member read out a nine-point allegation of misconduct and corruption regarding an important committee in the congregation. The work of this committee was central to the forward progress of the congregation through their transition. And while the work of this particular committee was entirely confidential, the member making these accusations clearly had received various bits of factual information in order to compile the allegations of misconduct. In fact, the confidentiality leaks were great enough to lend credibility to the accusations.

Yet none of the nine points were true. Just as Nehemiah had letters from the king in his possession authorizing the work of rebuilding the walls, this transitional pastor had confidential documents entirely refuting the nine points of accusation. Just as Nehemiah was in the room when the king decided to allow the rebuilding of Jerusalem, this transitional pastor had been in the room when the alleged corruption was supposed to have taken place, and he knew that nothing at all like what was being alleged had happened.

Rarely is there enough time to think through the various options of responding when accusations fly up in the heat of the moment. This transitional leader managed to not break any of the confidences that secured the refuting information. He did not proceed through a point-by-point refutation of the nine allegations. He simply said, "I am aware of all of the dynamics of this situation, and while the proceedings of this committee are all confidential, I can assure you that none of the things you have said are true."

That was not the end of the trouble. Someone willing to make false accusations is usually willing to repeat false accusations even when a trustworthy person in possession of all the facts has denied the truth of the accusations. The accuser lashed out with several letters repeating the falsehoods and further damage control was necessary. Unable to gain traction, the accuser finally left.

Countering Rumors

In order to lead well every leader must have some level of empathy for people—some amount of emotional connection to others. An emotionally connected leader will be attached at some non-rational level to friend and enemy alike. So of course Nehemiah was hurt, upset, distracted, and fearful when he read the letter from Sanballat containing false rumors. And yet, for the sake of the work and for the sake of his own well-being he needed to detach from that emotional connection.

When the announcement is made that the pastor is leaving the collective imagination of all of the people in the congregation is suddenly opened to a dizzying array of possibilities. A state of imaginative instability possesses the church's emotions due to the open question of who will lead this organization into the future. Since a transitional pastor is by nature the agent of a dynamic and wildly unknown future, and since a transitional pastor is usually a mostly unknown person to the congregation, rumors tending toward personally undermining the integrity of the transitional pastor are likely to rise up and circulate to some extent. Good communication practices blunt the forces of rumor. Constant spiritual practices of prayer, meditation, and worship are essential to countering the discouragement of rumors.

Handling the Corruption of Friends

Friends can be a refuge in times of difficulty. Yet transitional pastors often serve at some distance from their home communities and their friends. It is important to take time to nurture longer-term friendships, even if that means taking time away from the community where you serve. And as the opening scene of this book suggested, as I portrayed a conversation between a new interim pastor and a friend who was more experienced, a phone friendship with another transitional pastor can be a way to face challenging situations armed with reflective advice and emotional support.

Friendships will develop with staff members and with people in the congregation. Wariness is not the best stance when developing new friendships, yet it is essential to be professionally watchful as those friendships unfold.

Attacks are more emotionally effective when they come from friends. This reality might move a person toward isolation. Instead a more spiritually mature approach to friendships is warranted. In most cases the interim pastor will be in relationship with the people in the community for a short, yet intense period of time. A certain amount of closeness is inherent in all pastoral relationships. But a measure of reserve is wise when so much is taking place. No rule of thumb could possibly guide in this process. Yet a certain amount of intentional reflection on the depth of friendship and on the emotional vulnerability inherent in the role of transitional pastor is wise.

The battle is not always against someone out there. The battle with discouragement is often a battle with yourself. Self-control may sometimes mean deliberately choosing to do something difficult. Or it may entail a choice to refrain from doing something when internal or external pressure to act begins to drive decisions.

9

Time to Refrain

Luke 10:1–24
John 20:21
Leadership Narrative in Acts

I was home from college for the summer. One day my older brother pulled up to our house at lunchtime in his delivery truck. He opened the door to the cab of the truck and out bounded a beautiful three-month-old yellow Labrador puppy. When the pup came and placed his head in my paws for a good rub, my brother said, "Do you want him?"

I was confused and surprised, so I cannot remember if anything came out of my mouth. My brother went on to tell me that a co-worker of his was going into the Air Force so he could not keep this puppy. He was trying to find the dog a home.

I looked back toward the pup. "We would have to convince Dad."

"We can do that," my brother said. And then I thought of the chickens, rabbits, fish, cats, and stray dogs our parents had tolerated over the years. Other than snakes our parents had proven to be irrationally tolerant of all the animals we brought into their lives.

My brother was right. Who could pass on a dog like this? "I think I'll name him Buddy," I said.

Buddy was the smartest dog I ever knew. Labradors are born with an eagerness to please to go along with a love of fetching things and all of the equipment and desire to be strong swimmers. Their feet are webbed for strong paddling in the water and their tails act like a rudder. I would throw sticks into the river and Buddy would swim out to get them.

Buddy loved all kinds of fetching games and he even invented a few of his own. He would sit while I would hide tennis balls all over our back yard. Then I would give him the signal to start searching. He would quickly range all over until he found every ball and brought them all back to where I stood. But one day, after all of the balls had been found, I had to go do something for a minute. When I came back all of the balls were missing. I stood for a moment trying to figure out what was going on. Buddy bounded around a little bit and I realized he was gesturing to me that he had hidden the balls for me and it was my turn to go find them. I walked the perimeter of the yard and soon had all of the balls back at his feet. As much as I was teaching Buddy, Buddy was teaching me.

Early in December our first chance arrived to transition Buddy from fetching sticks and balls and get him to plunge into the water to bring back a duck. A few of my friends and I headed to one of our favorite duck blinds on the Columbia River. None of us owned a boat, and I was the only one who had a retrieving dog, so our success that day entirely depended on the ability of Buddy to comprehend that a duck floating along on the river was the same sort of thing as a stick or tennis ball that I might throw in for him to retrieve. I was confident that Buddy would do it because he loved to swim, he loved to retrieve, and he always managed to understand my intentions when I would try to teach him a new thing.

We arrived before first light and hauled our decoys out to the river, setting them to float a few yards away from the cover of our blind. The air was crisp but not too frigid. Everything along the river was breathtakingly beautiful. But whatever ducks we did see flew by miles away. The plaintive pleading of our duck calls and our decoys placidly floating in the river's current failed to lure in any ducks.

On this particular cold yet windless day, with just the right combination of friends sitting in the duck blind, with Buddy calmly resting at my feet, and with a thermos full of soup, I was nearly content to accept a duckless day. Yet I was disappointed that my dog was missing his chance to show off his water retrieval skills.

We must have been enjoying the contents of our thermoses too much. A flock of ducks was suddenly over us without any of us noticing they were coming. We all stood up too hastily, aimed our shotguns, and fired before anyone had a chance to think. A lot of lead passed harmlessly around the ducks, giving them quite a scare I'm sure, but missing rather badly. One lone duck dropped from the sky. Ben yelled, "I got 'em," and we all scurried out of the blind to have a look.

The duck was motionless in the water about 30 yards off shore, drifting downstream at a lazy pace. I looked down at Buddy. His eyes were locked on the duck but he was making no move toward the water. "Go get 'em Buddy!" I shouted.

Buddy ran toward the edge of the water and stopped. He turned his head back at me and stared. "Go get 'em Buddy," I repeated, this time gesturing my arm toward the duck. For a split second he made like he was going in. He took a few steps into the water, then backed out again and looked at me.

"Is your dog going to get my duck?" Ben asked.

"I'm sure he will. He gets sticks and tennis balls all of the time," I answered, not feeling nearly as confident as my voice sounded.

We moved down shore a few steps to stay parallel with the drifting duck. Buddy kept watching the duck but he would not go in the river. I had never seen him pass up a chance to swim. We tried throwing sticks out near the duck in the hope that he would go in after the stick and then grab the duck, but that didn't work.

Two things weighed on me as I came to accept that Buddy was not going to swim out after the duck. First, I had brought my friends on this hunt with a promise that my dog would get their ducks. And second, I have a serious ethical problem with hunting or fishing and not eating the game once it is killed. I looked at Ben, and I looked at the duck out there drifting lifelessly in the current, and I made a decision. "I'm going to swim out there and get it," I said.

We continued to move down shore as I listened to the objections of my friends. The river was far too cold, they said. It wasn't safe, they argued. I would get hypothermia or cramp up or something, they worried. I responded with reason. The duck was not that far off shore. People do polar bear swims in the dead of winter and this was not nearly as cold. I would turn around and come back without the duck if I felt any cramping coming on. I had more reasons than they had objections.

The duck floated farther downstream. I stripped down to nothing and waded out into the water. There was no point in hesitating. I launched out, keeping my head out of the water so that I would not get my hair wet. The water was cold but manageable and in no time I was standing back on shore with the duck in hand. It was cold but I was soon dressed again in all of my heavy clothes and Ben was handing me a cup of chicken noodle soup from his thermos.

Buddy had watched my every move. I found myself wondering if by watching me he had learned how to go out and retrieve the next duck. But then I realized he had learned a different lesson. That day I taught Buddy that if he waited long enough he would not have to go into the cold water to get anything floating out there because I would be happy to go out and get it myself.

*   *   *

Pastors develop a complex unspoken agreement with their congregations about what they will and will not do. This involves so many issues it would be impossible to even begin a list. Most of these agreements are tacit, implied by the actions and reactions of congregation and pastor in a multitude of interactions. *What does the congregation do for itself? What does the pastor do for the congregation? And what does the congregation do for the pastor?*

One pastor lived in a manse next to the church. He had a German Shepherd dog and he loved to walk through the building every night with his dog, making sure all of the doors to the church were locked. Even though he was a highly successful leader of a medium-sized church with several staff members, he liked to be the one to check the doors every night. He also took great joy when the building was clean and in good shape, so he was known to use the church's carpet cleaning machine from time to time to clean the carpets.

When that pastor was called on to another church a significant amount of effort was needed to find someone willing to look after the building in these ways.

Transitional pastors are often immediately confronted with requests to take up the long list of things the previous pastor voluntarily did. If the previous pastor was a computer expert, the first time something is wrong with one of the church's computers the new pastor will be regarded as the one to fix it. One of the primary tasks of a transitional pastor is to endure the embarrassment of awkward incompetence. The image of the previous pastor often lives on in the minds of the people as a basic measurement of pastoral worth. To refuse to shampoo the carpets or to be incapable of fixing a computer glitch becomes evidence that the transitional pastor is less of a pastor.

This is not merely a lamentable reality. By bearing the awkward embarrassment of these moments and continuing to provide good leadership, the transitional pastor is actually accomplishing a task. These moments encourage the congregation relinquish unreasonable expectations and begin to embrace a future with a new pastor.

Yet more than just those unreasonable expectations need to be relinquished. The way the previous pastor went about doing the many tasks of ministry is deeply engrained into the fabric of what is expected of the transitional leader. A host of seemingly insignificant items form the fabric of everyone's basic sense of what is expected of them and how they get their jobs done. None of the previous answers to any of these questions are settled when the church is going through a leadership change.

Transitional pastors must lead with sensitivity toward both the need for continuity and the need for change. Continuity is necessary because people who are feeling a bit anxious about the changes happening in the church as the familiar pastor has left need some stability. But also, a congregation that is about to welcome a new pastor will inevitably be accepting some other changes, and too many changes can be counterproductive. Yet some changes are necessary to prepare for new leadership.

So how much change should a transitional pastor bring? Changes that grow organically out of the needs of the people and their passion for extending the mission of the congregation are good. Changes that grow from within the perspective of the transitional pastor or out of an inner need to affect the direction the congregation is moving will ultimately become at least a distraction and at worst an impediment for the next pastor. You can coach people in their passions for new ministry initiatives. You can provide a framework for extending the best elements of the church's past. You can build a foundation for future growth. But you cannot get the duck for them.

Consider the episode in the gospels when Jesus sends out the seventy on a mission. Luke 10:1–24 narrates a rather surprising event considering the relative inexperience of the general group of the followers of Jesus at this stage. Jesus trains thirty-five pairs of people to go ahead of him and engage in the mission. These verses suggest multiple applications, but I am highlighting this episode to point to just one thing. If these relatively new followers of Jesus can be trusted to engage in mission without having him around, surely a church between pastors can be trusted to engage in the mission of Jesus without waiting for the next ministry vision. This time of refraining from certain initiatives is most definitely not a time for suspending engagement in service and outreach. It is a time for letting the natural mission impulses of the community emerge and lead.

In the time between pastors the congregation is finding it-self—finding its new equilibrium, finding its voice, finding new initiatives in the absence of the previous pastor. This work of discovery is uncomfortable, yet crucial for the future. In light of the demands of this work it is important to know when to refrain from the strong leadership style that may have been very effective for you in previous leadership situations.

John 20:21 presents one of the most startling statements among the things Jesus said to his disciples. "And again Jesus said, "Peace be with you! As the Father has sent me, I am sending you."

In some very fundamental ways the people of any church are the heirs of that commission. The hope is that the next pastor will have a positive influence on the church's ability to live fully in their identity as the people who have been sent to serve the world in their particular location and time just as the Father sent Jesus to serve the world. Whenever this church in transition happens to get their next pastor it will be best if that pastor finds them thoroughly engaged in the mission that has been laid on their hearts.

The book of Acts describes a church infused with this kind of energy. Luke narrates certain events featuring the initiatives of the apostles followed by spontaneous and unauthorized counterpoint events. In Acts 1:15–26 the apostles select Matthias to replace Judas, bringing the number of apostles back up to twelve. This episode has all of the marks of a conservative and institutional approach to church leadership. A slot has opened up on the committee so a meandering pathway of reasoning identifies a particular person to fill that slot. The reasoning is all sound, and everything is done in humility and in a prayerful spirit. No criticism of this approach is ever raised. Yet Acts 9:1–30 narrates a highly contrasting account of the conversion and deployment of Saul. Against the objections of the institutional leader (Acts 9:13–14), and without consulting the highest levels of the hierarchy (Acts 9:26), Paul begins his lifelong engagement in the mission of preaching (Acts 9:19–22). A similar pattern is recorded in the response to a problem with the distribution of food and the response of the apostles in forming a committee to address the concern (Acts 6:1–6). Two of the institutional choices for the limited task of food distribution, Stephen and Philip, crash through the boundaries of their institutional assignment and become powerful, yet unauthorized preachers (Acts 6:8–7:53; Acts 8:4–13, 25–40). In each case the institutional leaders eventually catch up with, bless, and authorize the work of these breakout leaders (Acts 8:14, 10:34–35, 15:1–31).

The initial apostolic pattern—the reasonable method of considering options and prayerfully selecting leaders for the people of a church—will most likely describe the methods used to select the next pastor of the church. At the same time, breakout leaders will push beyond the expectations for their roles. A congregation in transition will be a place of spiritual health and energetic expansion if passionate people are fully engaged in the central mission of that particular church in that particular location. Breakout leaders emerge in an environment where the institutional leaders proactively engage in mission while at the same time refrain from excessive control of the emerging initiatives that stretch beyond the established boundaries.

Case Study: the Speaker Conundrum

A congregation had received a monetary gift to pay for an annual youth retreat. This congregation aspired to bring in high quality speakers for this annual event and this gift made that financially feasible. While at a pastor's conference the pastor heard a very engaging speaker who was nationally prominent in the area of youth ministry. After the speaker's talk was finished the pastor approached the speaker and inquired if she would be available to come speak at the youth retreat. At the time the youth retreat was scheduled for about eight months in the future. Though this speaker was in high demand, the scheduled weekend just happened to be free in the speaker's schedule. A very thoughtful conversation took place between the speaker and the pastor about the goals of the youth weekend and both were excited about what could happen at the event.

A committee at the church was responsible for making all of the arrangements for the retreat. They met with the speaker by conference call a few times and discussed the format for the weekend and some of the speaker's topics. All was going well.

About four months before the scheduled date of the weekend youth retreat the pastor announced he was taking a call at another church. Leadership of the planning team for the retreat shifted to one of the youth leaders. While it seemed a little daunting to go on with the retreat in the absence of a pastor, no one felt any compelling reason to cancel the speaker or the event.

About six weeks before the date of the retreat the congregation was in a short period after the previous pastor had left and before the interim pastor had arrived. The planning team leader—we will call him Jim—had a phone conversation with the speaker and enthusiastically took thorough notes of all the details and plans for the weekend. Jim wanted the planning team to know about all of the things that were discussed so he copied his notes of the phone conversation and distributed them to the rest of the planning team. Suddenly, within the space of two weeks the retreat planning team became entangled in such a divisive conflict that the retreat had to be cancelled. The presenting issue of the conflict was a disagreement over one controversial point in the speaker's presentation, along with a differing philosophy about how to handle worship at a youth retreat.

A few weeks later the interim pastor arrived on the scene and the appearance of reconciliation took place. But within six months the youth leader, Jim, who had been leading the planning team for the retreat quietly left for another congregation.

All of the people on the planning team were very good friends before this problem erupted. And the controversial point in the speaker's presentation was not a matter of doctrine, nor was it essential to the overall plan of the weekend. So why did this minor point of disagreement erupt?

The reports of Jim and the other main person involved in the conflict point to several factors.

This other person involved—let's call her Beth—wrote, "I think just the fact that we didn't have any pastor at the time was a big part of the trouble. Normally a pastor would have stepped in and met with people and patched it up. Had the new interim pastor been with us by the time of the controversy, though she knew nothing about what had happened, she would have been able to sort things out."

Anger played a large part in the volatile nature of the interactions. According to one of the reports, the anger arose out of feelings of having been deceived. The pastor had invited the speaker, but he was now gone. The youth leader, Jim, who had taken over leadership of the planning team was, in a way, filling in the place of the pastor. When the controversial topic was revealed, Jim responded positively to the challenges inherent in a controversial topic. But Beth, who took exception, felt deceived. This topic and the way it was being presented fell far outside the stated purpose of the retreat in the mind of Beth, who then grew angry about the apparent deceptiveness. She initiated a phone conversation with the speaker. During the phone call Beth had raised objections to the particular point and to the format for worship, but the speaker stated that when she and the pastor had originally discussed the topics for the retreat, this controversial topic and this particular way of presenting the topic had been discussed.

But the pastor was no longer present. Beth had no way to ask, "Did you know it would be this way when you arranged for this speaker?"

This may provide a clue to the reaction of anger. Might it be that Beth was really angry with the pastor for leaving? Was this anger being transferred to Jim when he took over the leadership of planning the retreat and symbolically took the pastor's place? In this interaction the response of anger led to several ripples of reaction through the planning team.

At a critical point in the development of the conflict Beth took the controversial youth retreat topic to other committees of the congregation, asking them to weigh in. It is clear from the reports that this episode led to the strengthening of one power coalition in the church family system. A script was developed—perhaps not consciously—of what to do to resist any kind of change when it is uncomfortable. A pattern of procedure emerged to bounce uncomfortable ideas around the various committees of the church as a way of putting a stop to all initiatives. This pattern was repeated for the next two decades.

Paradoxically, good transitional leadership under these circumstances means assertively reducing the power of institutionally rigid coalitions within the organization. This is paradoxical because effort must be exerted in order to help the institution to refrain from undue control. Refraining should be seen as leaving room for the absence created by the interim between pastors to be filled by people stepping forward in response to the leading of the Holy Spirit.

It must be noted that these observations are only valid in the context of church community that tends toward the preservation of order over and against the sometimes-chaotic outbursts of breakout movements. Some congregations cultivate a culture favoring innovation and missional experimentation. At their best these congregations excel in deploying people rapidly in mission. Yet those groups may waste a great deal of energy in unwise bursts of activity with no real planning and with no cohesive vision of the purpose of new initiatives. Congregations on this end of the spectrum may need help refraining from too many scattered outbursts of disorganized mission initiative.

Transitional leaders in churches on either end of this spectrum should embrace the most obvious advantage of a temporary leader: you are temporary. The credibility of a transitional leader is greater in one way than any other type of pastor. In certain ways a transitional leader can make penetrating and uncomfortable observations about unhealthy and unproductive patterns in the congregational system without appearing to have an ulterior motive. At the right time, in the right setting, with the right people present, a transitional pastor might say, "As a person who has recently come to this congregation from outside, I am noticing some patterns of interaction that are holding you back from becoming all that you could be. As you know, I am not here for a long time. I don't stand to gain anything from making these observations. In fact, because I love you so much it is painful for me to have to call your attention to this. But I would be doing a disservice if I did not tell you plainly what I see. At times, individuals and groups have a habit of . . . "

The advantage here lies in the hands of the transitional leader because this is clearly not an effort to limit the control of one group for the sake of advancing his or her own power. This leadership instead amounts to assertively causing the organization to refrain from its own debilitating patterns so that the next pastor will have more space to create new patterns and healthy interactions in the future.

One interim pastor once said, "There is nothing so wrong with any congregation that can't be fixed by ten good funerals."

That observation came out of the mouth of this particular interim pastor at a low moment in the battle against entrenched coalitions. He was lamenting the tendency of powerful groups within this congregation to immediately react to certain kinds of initiatives with a nearly robotic squelching pattern. He need not have assessed the situation in such a negative way. In fact, observations over time show that this interim pastor managed to begin the process of reducing the power of those very groups while also bringing the causes for their behavior to the surface. This healing of some of the dysfunction at work in the system took time, but things did improve dramatically over the next seven years without any of those ten particular funerals taking place. One decade after the "ten funerals" comment the senior pastor of the congregation said, "I have never served a congregation as healthy as this one in all of my years of ministry."

As people look backward and react to dynamics of their past they will find it difficult to energetically engage in the mission of the church. Carefully search for any evidence of a change in this state. When time passes and people respond to fill gaps in the church's mission important signs of change will begin to emerge. Signs of a change in relation to the mission are signs that they are beginning to be ready to move on toward healing.

10

Moving toward Healing

Mark 4
The Story of Jonah

It is dark, and you have been sent on a boat out onto the lake. Your friends are with you and when the wind rises and the waves start lapping over the sides of the gunwales, you all start to panic. But then you remember that Jesus is in the boat. He is sleeping. That seems tremendously unnatural. Your panic is moving toward the edge of terror.

Your terror is completely reversed in a short period of time. Jesus is awakened. He speaks to the storm, and the wind and waves immediately calm down. But still, there you are, sailing in the dark. The power Jesus wields is more terrifying than the storm.

How did you come to this moment—this overwhelming, crushing, and yet liberating existence between great terror and great faith? The day had started peacefully enough. Jesus sat in this very boat and taught people who were sitting on the shore, using the lake as his amphitheater, his voice ringing clearly across the ripples of the water. His images were full of life and hope—seeds growing, and a lamp image that cheered the hearts of poor people who struggled with fears of the dark.

Following that teaching filled with images of life and health, he sent you out on the lake you love so well. The lake is your source of food and your livelihood. And yet it is a dangerous lake. Storms come from nowhere, sometimes taking the lives of all who are caught out on the waters, regardless of their experience or skill. And this episode—this calming of the storm—is just the beginning. From here you will move through a series of three more miracles. Jesus will demonstrate his power over the most terrifying forces of death. He will heal a demon-possessed man who lives in the graveyard. While traveling to the next place you will encounter a man named Jairus who will be pleading with Jesus for his daughter's life. Jesus will go to help, but he will be maddeningly slow in getting there. On the way a woman who has struggled for fourteen years watching her life ebb away in a ceaseless flow of blood will touch the hem of his robe and he will feel the life-giving power flow from him. He will stop and have a conversation about a miracle that is already over and done, all the while casually delaying the excursion to save the life of Jairus's daughter. When he finally does arrive at the house of Jairus he will be too late to save her from death, but that will not matter. He will raise her anyway.

These four miracle stories overturn the four points the human terror compass: natural disaster, internal chaos, wasting illness, and death of a child. Taken together they signal a complete and total mastery over the forces of death and destruction. This sequence of narration identifies Jesus completely with that great and generous power to heal in the heart of God.

The first episode in this sequence—the story of a boat out on a storm—is in very close parallel to the first chapter of Jonah.[1] Detail by detail the events of these two stories line up in a precise parallel sequence. For example, God sent Jonah to a people outside of Israel. When Jesus said, "Let us go over to the other side," (Mark 4:35) he initiated a journey outside of the people of Israel. God had told Jonah, "Go to the great city of Nineveh . . ." (Jonah 1:2) but he got in a boat and went the other way. The friends of Jesus were on their way, obediently going in the right direction when, "A furious

---

1. Edwards, *Mark*, 149.

squall came up, and the waves broke over the boat, so that it was nearly swamped" (Mark 4:37). Not so different from the description of what happened to the boat Jonah was on. "Then the Lord sent a great wind on the sea, and such a violent storm arose that the ship threatened to break up" (Jonah 1:4).

The parallels continue and they are too close to be random convergences.

When we come to the height of each storm, with each parallel sleeper now awake and looking out at the wind and the waves, the central divergence occurs. Jesus rebuked the wind (Mark 4:39) but Jonah had the sailors pick him up and throw him into the sea (Jonah 1:11–12).

These are very different actions in the face of the storm, but the result is similar. "Then the wind died down and it was completely calm" (Mark 4:39). "Then they took Jonah and threw him overboard, and the raging sea grew calm" (Jonah 1:15).

All of pastoral ministry must point people to the goodness of God.

That is hard. It is complicated because we ourselves are likely to be aware of the terror in the waves. Our attention is likely to be fixed on the destructive potential of the wind. We spend most of our time afraid of what is happening rather than confidently rejoicing in the goodness of what God is doing. Sometimes we do not even know how to name the goodness of God within the hopelessness of how life feels.

On top of that, we are speaking of the goodness of God to people who are certain that the world is dangerous and out of control. Any word of hope is automatically filed in the category of foolish and unfounded optimism. We are given a message to share. "The world is full of trouble and God is saving us in the midst of that trouble." How does that not sound like sunny avoidance of reality or even dangerous ignorance?

Yet Jesus persisted, speaking life-giving words into the chaos and death all around him.

The Church Out on the Water

We want some dry land time, but the church has more often felt like it is out to sea. We somehow expect that the day will come when we can settle down on dry land. But that is not where the fish are. We are asked to believe that Jesus sees the storm, and he still wants us out there on the sea.

After this storm episode, and after the three subsequent episodes of death defying miracles, time goes by, maybe several months, and then a moment comes when some of the religious leaders ask Jesus to give them a miraculous sign.

Even though Jesus had performed miracles, faith cannot just be about on-demand miracles. So Jesus said, "For as Jonah was three days and three nights in the belly of a huge fish, so the Son of Man will be three days and three nights in the heart of the earth" (Matt 12:40).

Just as Jonah was thrown into the chaos of the storm as an offering, so Jesus offered himself to be thrown into the chaos of our whole world gone wrong. And here is the resolution of all the great paradoxes swirling around our storm—our great storm—the storm of humanity's big dilemma. Jesus is responsible for it because he is responsible for everything. He is not aloof to the dangers. He is right in the middle of it all. Jesus ultimately throws his own self into the chaos of the storm to bring us safely to the other shore. Pastoral ministry means having our attention firmly fixed on his goodness as we walk with people from their land of brokenness and suffering into the place of his goodness.

I know that is true, and yet I lose my grip on that truth so often. I may be afraid of the intimacy of getting so close to people in order to serve as their pastor. I may be afraid of my own weakness and inability in light of the enormous tasks. I may be overwhelmed by the chaos. I may have my attention arrested by the wind and the waves and I may think Jesus is asleep.

Pastoral ministry begins in the goodness of God and is sustained by the power of the one who made everything good. But I remain who I am—one who treads water on the edge of the larger realities.

Healing Broken Bones

When I was a kid a man once told me the story of when he broke his wrist as a child. For two days his parents did not think the wrist was really broken but when he was still in great pain on the third day they took him to a doctor. The doctor informed them that the wrist really was broken. To make matters worse the bones of the wrist were askew, and in the three days since the break the bones had already begun healing in the wrong position. The wrist would need to be re-broken and then set in the correct position if they were to hope for it to heal properly. My friend then shared that this happened right before the development of modern anesthesia so that the only available means to put him to sleep was ether. Ether definitely brings deep sleep but the patient can still feel the pain in dreams. In order to stop the twisted chaos of the dislocated bones healing together at bad angles, the doctor had to take this boy through a painful and disruptive journey. The bones needed to be violently reset. Years later, as he was telling me the story, he held up his wrist and showed me the full range of motion in the wrist.

Most of the time it hurts to stop what has twisted the joy out of the church's life. The healing that comes in church leadership transitions is often like setting broken bones. How can a transitional pastor be a life-affirming force of healing and restoration during a short duration of ministry?

Many have written about the congregation as an emotional system. In his book, *How Your Church Family Works*, Peter Steinke gives some foundational thoughts for understanding the patterns of interaction for people in an emotional system. "System theory focuses on how interactions are mutually influenced and how they become *patterned* or repeated."[2] A narrative analysis of the congregational system will identify a plot in the construction of

2. Steinke, *How Your Church Family Works*, 6.

patterned interactions. Smaller stories within the larger narrative will reveal how the patterns of interaction came to be and how they changed over time through the stalemates of certain conflicts or the victories of the prevailing point of view. Narratives about the leadership of previous pastors will emerge as part of why the system is the way it is. These narratives might turn out to be the story of why diverse people got along well in the past through the skillful leadership of previous pastors. Or the interventions of previous pastors may have left wounded individuals scraping for some measure of control, as their voices were continually unheard. Both of these narrative extremes may surface about the very same pastor.

Think about individuals in the system and then also think about a system of individuals. How can you bring healing to the hurting individuals in the system, and how can you bring healthier functioning to the system as a whole in a short amount of time? The blended details from several different interactions at several different churches formed the following case study.

The Sunday School Hour: a Composite Case Study

Greg was working in his office on a Wednesday morning in August when Christine knocked on his door and asked to have a few moments. "Actually, it won't take just a few moments. If I told you everything it would take hours."

Christine was one of the most hardworking and dedicated children's ministries directors Greg had ever worked with, but he has aware of some friction in the children's ministries program. He had some time available in his schedule so he decided now would be as good of a time as any to dive into that area of conflict. "I have some time now, and if we don't get to everything we can schedule a time to meet again later," he said as he invited her to sit at the table across from him in his office.

Part of how Christine did such an excellent job with the few hours she was paid to work with children per week lay in the speed of her internal metronome. She always was thinking and moving a little faster than everyone else, multi-tasking and pushing aside irrelevant details as she made her way straight to the point. But Greg could sense the speed of her thoughts was racing beyond the usual pace. She was agitated. Nervous energy was pouring out all over. "So much happened before you came here, so I don't really know where to begin. This is all about what took place while I was on vacation at the start of the month. Do you want to hear about the problem, or do you want me to go back and tell the whole history? If I do that it is going to take a while."

"I think it is important for me to know as much as I can learn about the interactions in the past. But why don't you first tell me the immediate problem."

"Okay, well as you know I was only gone for two Sundays. I had someone from the Christian education team serve as temporary superintendent while I was gone. When I came in to work on Monday morning I had an email saying that she won't ever serve again as temporary superintendent. I don't know what I am going to do because if I don't have someone to walk the little ones down to the children's classroom area when they are let out of worship I won't ever be able to be gone on a Sunday."

"You don't have anyone else who might be trained to fill in?"

"No, I have lots of people who have filled in before, but no one will do it again. The trouble is this person, this one person, who always shows up when I am not back there and tries to take over. She's not even one of our teachers or on the Christian education team."

"Can't you talk with her and explain that all of the people working in the children's area need to be part of the team, or there for a reason?"

Christine's eyes grew even more agitated, and Greg could detect that she was even shaking a bit. "Oh boy," she said. "I'm really going to have to tell you the whole thing."

The church had been founded in a quaint little building that was very attractive in a number of ways but entirely inadequate for children and youth programs. For years the congregation went around and around as they considered selling the building and moving to a new location without ever coming to any conclusions.

Christine narrated this whole story. Greg knew all of these details but he listened patiently, allowing Christine to make her way to the part he did not yet know. He sensed she was coming to the relevant details when she said one name: Marianne.

Marianne had been instrumental in those years as the volunteer leader of the children's ministry. She found ways of improvising so that the complete lack of space never seemed like a problem to anyone in the congregation. She creatively planned events for kids, sometimes even held in her own home, or she would use the worship space in off hours for Sunday school.

This all worked fine when the congregation was small. But twelve years ago a new pastor arrived with a set of skills highly conducive to growth. Within eighteen months of his arrival the number of people attending every week grew to the point that the worship space was overcrowded. While most people were supportive of adding a second service, Marianne was not. A congregational meeting was held to discuss the changes needed and several people showed up who had not been attending very regularly. They were very much opposed to adding a new service. The pastor had noticed, as he later told Christine, how all of the people who showed up at the meeting to oppose adding the service were friends of Marianne.

"What was so bad about adding a second service that she would call all of her friends and get them to show up at a congregational meeting?" Greg asked Christine.

"I don't think anyone knew at the time. No one apparently gave any compelling reasons for not going forward with a second service, but the plan was modified based on Marianne's . . . requirements."

Christine spit out that last word—requirements—like it was a bad piece of food. "Requirements . . . ?" was all Greg had to say.

"Well back then Marianne got whatever she wanted. She did so much that people were scared to ever oppose her on anything. She had an annual Christmas pageant that took up most of the month of December for everyone in the church, and everyone loved it. They say the place was packed whenever any children's program was performed. She really had a lot going on. Just not what I would do. So she didn't like the Sunday morning schedule for two services the way it was originally proposed. They were going to have services at 9:30 and 11:00 but she said that would make it impossible to hold Sunday school, and with the way the building was back then, she was right. So they put the first service at 8:30 and the second service at 11:00 with Sunday school from 9:45 to 10:45. Everything took a dive at that point. Not very many people wanted to come to worship at 8:30, so the first service didn't go well. Not many people wanted to bring their kids for Sunday school at 9:45 so that didn't go well, and 11:00 was a little late for families to stay. Kids would get hungry for lunch, everyone was cranky, so a church that had been having a hard time fitting everyone in for one service suddenly saw a drop in everything—attendance, giving, participation in mission projects—it was a huge step back."

"Yeah, I've seen that in the annual statistics. I was kind of wondering what happened in that year," Greg said.

"Steve wasn't the kind of pastor who would let that go on for long," Christine said, looking a little less anxious. "I would imagine he met with Marianne right away to try to negotiate a different set up. But isn't that weird? Even as I say it I think, *here he is, the pastor of the church, and he has to go to her like he is a little kid asking permission to go to the bathroom.* But that's the way it was. And she loved it. I don't think she cared about the kids so much as it was her way to have power. Anyway, she wouldn't compromise on anything. And at that point she didn't need to, because here is the other factor. Her mother, you've never met her, right? She is in a care facility now, but Marianne's mother, Phyllis, used to run everything on the board of elders. Whatever Marianne wanted for children's ministries, Phyllis would make happen through the elders. But then: term limits. She had to go off because she had been on for six years."

Christine unwittingly allowed the slightest flash of a grin to cross her lips as she came to the part about how Marianne and Phyllis's power had been thwarted. But the grin disappeared as she continued on.

"And that is when Pastor Steve saw his chance. You know that old strip mall across from where the church used to be? Well Pastor Steve swung a deal to rent out space there on Sunday mornings, so that Sunday School could happen during the worship service. Without getting "permission" from Marianne, the elders rented that space and moved the time of the services to 9:00 and 10:30 and held Sunday school during the 10:30 hour in that other facility. And things just took off from there. They were instantly up in everything—finances, attendance—and that is when the new building campaign started. That is how we got this building we are in today, because Pastor Steve saw his way of getting around Phyllis and Marianne."

"How did she react?"

"Well, see, that is part of how he was able to get things like that done. Pastor Steve was always one step ahead. Before the subject of renting out the space in that strip mall ever even came up he was already talking with me about a job. I was finishing with college at the time and even though this church had never had a paid children's ministries director before, he would ask me from time to time if I might be interested. I was getting a degree in early childhood education but I wasn't so sure I wanted to be a teacher. My parents were friends of his family even though my family went to another church, so I knew him and he knew about me. The instant the elders rented out that space for children's ministries Marianne resigned her position of volunteer Sunday school superintendent in protest. She thought everyone would come running to her and ask what they had to do to win her back. But I think Pastor Steve knew she would do that and he was ready. Before anyone could even think of having Marianne come back they threw her a big retirement party and I had a job offer within a couple of weeks. So I ran that ministry out of the strip mall and then transitioned to what you see today when they bought the land and built this building."

"Wow, with all of that history it is kind of surprising that Phyllis and Marianne are still in this church."

"Yeah, they were never too happy with pastor Steve. When we got the news that he was moving on to that bigger congregation in California, it was about the worst day ever for most people, but I think Marianne probably drove over to her mother's care center and they high-fived each other that Sunday. But I think a lot of factors played into keeping them in our church. All of their friends are here, and they were in a position to move on to a new phase of life. Marianne was in good health and ready to retire, and not having Sunday School every week was probably a relief. But boy, she can't stand the sight of me."

Greg let out his breath and tried to release a little of the frustration he was feeling as he listened empathetically to Christine's story. "So from her point of view you represented the reason she was moved out of her place in this church. How did you handle being the target all of those years?"

"Well at first I almost couldn't handle it all. She did try to get me fired. It was an endless stream of complaints. Not all of them came from her, but she was behind most if not all of them. There was no consistency to it. First it was a complaint that one teacher was giving sugary treats to the kids, and that was somehow my fault. And then we were too rigorous about background checks for adults working with kids. Things like that. It all came to a head about two years after I started. One night Marianne and Phyllis and four of their friends showed up unannounced at a meeting of the board of elders. And they asked that I be asked to leave the room so they could *speak freely.*"

Greg watched as Christine raised her hands and scratched quotation marks in the air. Her fingers clearly had not forgotten the anger of that moment. "Did you leave?"

"Well, no. Fortunately Pastor Steve knew how to handle the situation. He stumbled around for a couple of minutes, because this thing just hit him right out of the blue. I could see the wheels turning as he was trying to say something coherent and not make anything worse. And then the light went on: personnel committee. He let them say the gist of what they had come for and then he said this was an employment issue, so it would not be right to listen to a complaint in an open meeting of the elders. So the personnel committee met with them, and met with me. It was all a big waste of time because things were going better with children's ministries than ever before."

Greg nearly commented, but he did not want to interrupt the story and soon Christine was telling more. "The thing was, I was told to change some things, but the personnel committee could see what was really going on. They sat down with Marianne and Phyllis and asked them to stay away from me and from the children's ministry. I don't think they said it that bluntly, and Marianne couldn't resist picking at me from time to time. But Pastor Steve would always watch to see if she was harassing me and he did talk to her from time to time. Now that he is gone I guess she thinks she can step up the attacks again."

* * *

In a deeply entrenched conflict like this, where several years have gone by and several layers of hurt have grown over the top of the initial disagreement, it seems impossible to imagine reconciliation. Benjamin Franklin is quoted as having said, "God heals, and the doctor takes the fees." If the wounds apparent in this conflict are going to be healed, it will have to be the work of God. Yet like a doctor assisting God in the healing process, a transitional pastor can engage in work for the sake of creating the conditions most likely to achieve healing.

As a transitional pastor, Greg is going to consider visiting with Marianne and Phyllis as a first step in bringing healing to this longstanding conflict.

Greg has an advantage. He is not a party to the conflict, and he was not involved when it got started. So far he has not done anything to make it worse. Yet in his role as pastor he may inherit residual bad feelings by a process of transference.

He will, of course, be tempted to believe he understands what happened based on what Christine has told him of the history. But he will be wise to begin by purging from his mind all confidence that he really knows what is going on.

One common technique used by writers of novels might suggest a pathway for pursuing a more complete understanding. Have you ever read a book in which the novelist gives an incomplete set of facts implying that one particular narrative is true? Then after leading the reader down a false road for a time, one more piece of information comes into the story. This last piece of information changes everything. Such is the possibility with Christine's story. Christine is an honest person and she sat in the front row while all of these events unfolded. Yet her story may well be missing some pieces of information that would completely change the narrative.

In fact, given this story I would expect that a visit to Phyllis and Marianne would reveal an entirely different perspective on the events narrated by Christine. A transitional leader must find a way to become "unknowing" about Christine's narrative. Greg cannot forget her story. He will come to any meeting with Phyllis and Marianne with set thoughts about what took place in the history of this conflict. Even his body will tense up when he hears the story from the side of the other people involved. While he listens to the events from the other side in the conflict he will form judgments. Yet a spiritual state of "unknowing," is possible. All conclusions may be put on hold or turned into tentative suppositions in more than merely an intellectual way. The most effective way of working toward this state comes in prayer. Greg should commit to twenty-four hours of prayer for Marianne and Phyllis prior to meeting with them. If Greg will pray for these two for twenty-four hours he will create the conditions whereby his outlook will be changed. He will grow receptive to hearing their story independently of how he perceives things following the narration by Christine.

Following a time of hearing Phyllis and Marianne's account an assessment should be made about how to proceed. This conflict has simmered for years with only an occasional boil over. While pastors can effectively just manage conflict, a pastoral transition represents an opportunity to bring healing.

A purely rational assessment of this deeply entrenched conflict could lead to a pragmatic decision that these relationships are deeply clouded by the past and any hope for reconciliation is very unrealistic. But the story of Jesus calming the storm on Galilee compels openness to the intrusion of a greater healing than any rational analysis might anticipate.

What leadership characteristics encourage this kind of healing? Confidentiality is imperative. Be a trustworthy person for hurting people to tell the stories of their hearts. It is tempting for a helping person to share information between two conflicting parties in the hope that if misunderstandings were corrected or if information or perspectives could go back and forth between the two parties, the conflict would go away. This kind of thinking is misguided and dangerous. Most conflicts are not based on a lack of information or a simple misunderstanding. Conflicts linger because people are hurting. In order to work towards healing a pastor needs to be a confidential person.

This kind of healing work can be intense, and it can require a great deal of time. It is important to maintain an even perspective on all of the underlying hurts you discover. Some things should be referred to a professional counselor for extended care. Some things can be accomplished by bringing in mediators, with the permission of the people involved. Some healing can only begin in the time frame available and you will have to trust it to continue beyond your involvement.

Followers of Jesus are walking in the footsteps of the one who calmed the seas and who identified himself in the sign of Jonah. That must mean something about how we engage in healing the chaos in the relationships of people in churches.

The image of Jesus calming the storm brings a certain kind of comfort. But Jesus did not calm every storm, just that one. What about the times when the storm does not stop and the ship goes down? Leading through shipwreck may be the more applicable metaphor in some situations. In the next chapter we turn our thoughts toward those times when disaster strikes.

11

Leading through Shipwreck

Acts 27:1—28:14

The whole story was as terrifying as any Hollywood disaster movie. Travelling on the Mediterranean Sea late in the year was dangerous. The cargo ship from Adramyttium bound for Italy carried several passengers along with the wheat in its holds. With some difficulty due to adverse winds the ship managed to sail to an area mostly protected from the prevailing winds called "Fair Havens" on the south side of the Island of Crete.

Among the passengers, a brilliant prisoner named Paul sailed on this long journey to Rome. He seemed to be the kind of person who knows a little something about everything and he never was intimidated by the expertise of others. As a prisoner of the state bound for the capital in Rome, he did not have much power when the centurion in charge of transporting him met with the pilot of the ship and the owner to discuss plans for waiting out the winter storms. Paul gave his opinion about the voyage in his typical brash style. Sailing on in these unpredictable conditions was likely to prove costly or even fatal. The experts disagreed.

Fair Havens was only a temporarily safe place. It was not the best place to be in the winter. Those in charge of making decisions favored sailing on just a little further east along the southern side of the island of Crete to try to reach a harbor town called Phoenix because it was a better place to spend the winter. The shape of the land there afforded greater protection from the winter winds.

Everything seemed to point in the direction of making a run for Phoenix when a moderate south wind gently began to blow, so the anchor was brought on board and soon they were underway, pushed along on the breath of that favorable wind. Hugging the southern coast of Crete, they made their way east. But then a huge storm blew in from the northeast. The sailors had no way to counter the force of the winds. The ship was blown out into open waters. A little island called "Cauda," just south of Crete became one of the last visible sights of dry land as the storm swept the ship south and westward. It was tremendously unnerving to watch the sailors wrestle with bringing the lifeboat onto the main ship. They could no longer keep it secure out on the waters. Next they passed ropes under the hull of the main ship in an effort to keep the whole thing from breaking apart. Navigation was no longer really possible. All they could do was drag a sea anchor to slow the speed at which the ship was being driven by the wind. Had they not slowed the ship against the wind they very well may have been driven all of the way south to Africa and run aground on the sandbars off the coast of present day Lybia.

By the next day things were so bad that they threw all of the cargo overboard, and by the day after that they threw some of the ship's equipment overboard. Day after day the storm blew. They neither saw the sun by day nor the stars by night for days on end. The constant violent motion of the ship stole everyone's appetite. This collection of sailors, soldiers, prisoners and passengers endured two weeks of constant stress without eating a thing. Floating around at the whim of the winds in an ancient ship, most of the people on board believed they were about to die. Starving, battered, completely without hope, huddled together in some part of the ship, they were surprised when Paul stood up to speak to them.

No one likes to hear "I told you so." I imagine a resounding groan arising from everyone when Paul began by telling them all that he warned this would happen. Or maybe they were so cowed by the storm that they simply listened. He then went on to promise every soul on board that they would live through this experience. The ship would go down, he said, but there would be no loss of life. In the night an angel had come to Paul and had predicted that he would get his chance to defend himself in court against the charges he was facing. The angel further promised that everyone on board would survive the shipwreck, that the ship would run aground on some island, and all would make it safely to land.

That night, as the ship drifted along, the sailors began to sense that some land was near. They had been out on open waters for so long. It had seemed like too much to hope for that they would ever make it to shore. Apparently enough equipment was left to measure the depth of the water underneath them. The first sounding indicated a depth of a little over 120 feet. As they moved along they measured again and the depth was now only ninety feet. The sailors saw their chance. They were the only ones on board in possession of the knowledge that the ship was being driven toward land. They also knew what everyone knew: the lifeboat was not big enough for everyone. Under the pretense of lowering more sea anchors they tried to lower the lifeboat into the sea and escape before anyone else on board might notice. And no one did notice, except Paul. He pointed out to the soldiers on board that everyone was doomed without the help of the sailors. If the sailors were gone no one else was going to make it through. So the soldiers cut the lines and the lifeboat drifted away.

The sky began to lighten in the east. Paul repeated the promise: all of them would live through the disaster. He urged them, once again, to eat. This time, though, he took a piece of bread, gave thanks, broke it, and began to eat. That simple series of actions means so much when narrated in just that order. Luke does not hit us over the head and overtly remind us of communion but those actions, narrated in that order, are meant to give courage to people who have lost hope.

This ship was bigger than I first imagined. In all, 276 people were on board. They all ate as much as they wanted and then threw the last of the provisions into the sea. The outlines of the land ahead became more distinct in the growing light, but no one knew exactly where they were. All they could see was a bay and a sandy beach so they cut all of the sea anchors in the hope that the wind would drive the ship on shore. This worked partially. They struck a sand bar and came to a halt. The force of the waves slammed into the stern and everything was breaking up.

How cheap was life in that culture. After all this, the soldiers were afraid that as the ship broke up some of the prisoners might escape. In order to prevent that they were planning to execute all of the prisoners, but their leader wanted for Paul to make it through so everyone was told to just make it to land by whatever means possible.

When the ship spit them out into the ocean near this unknown beach they had no idea what they would find if they managed to get to shore. What a contrast when they finally made it safely either by swimming or by grabbing onto a piece of the ship as is broke up underneath them—all 276 people on board. The inhabitants of the island, Malta, went into full Red Cross mode, providing what disaster assistance they could.

Paul must have been a highly energetic and restless person. We get that at times from some of his letters, but this trait is on full display in what happened next. Having been tossed around in a storm for two weeks with little food, and then having escaped the crashing waves and come to shore, in the cold and rain, Paul immediately began collecting wood for the fire. Others would have been hunkering down next to the fire with blankets over their heads, but not Paul. As he was laying the sticks on the fire a poisonous snake chomped down on his hand. The local islanders recognized what kind of snake this was. They knew the venom was fatal. They took this bad luck event as an omen of the great evil Paul must have perpetrated. What was this prisoner's crime? Cruel murder, no doubt. How else could this series of bad luck incidents be explained?

Paul gave a shake of his wrist and the snake met its doom in the fire. The locals knew what always happened next when someone was bitten by this kind of snake. They watched Paul for the onset of symptoms leading to death. But after enough time went by and Paul showed none of the signs they changed their minds and lauded Paul as a god.

Think of Paul as a transitional leader on this journey. Of course, he is not any kind of official leader at all. He is a prisoner. But even though he had no official leadership authority, yet the strength of his faith eventually propelled him to a point where he took over the entire operation. Transitional pastors walk a hard road because the sense of their authority within the hearts and minds of the people is often diminished for various reasons. Paul's example should teach us not to be daunted in the least by this aspect of the leadership challenge. Strong faith and bold leadership, sensitively asserted, is likely to yield good results. Even without sensitivity Paul managed pretty well.

Paul's passion for life meant that he became God's gift of life to people who would otherwise be lost. Everyone on board might have died at multiple points in the story were it not for the leadership he asserts.

Along the way Paul encountered opposition, but his steady assertion of hope and reason won people over.

Once on land the parallels between what Paul went through and the principles of transitional leadership continue. People are constantly looking for omens to bring order to the structure of their lives and systems of belief. In our world few people really believe that a shipwreck or hostile snake are signs of the vengeance of unseen spiritual forces. Some might admit to consulting their astrological chart every once in a while, but our scientific approach to the world has made us feel superior to the naïve Maltese we read about in this story. Yet people who are going through change put a great deal of trust in signs. The incident involving the snake is instructive. People undergoing the stress of change will take opposition or adversity as a sign that God is trying to prevent them from going forward. Roadblocks are commonly interpreted as God's way of telling us not to proceed.

Many of the people who surround a transitional leader will be judging whether God is in the plan based on the levels of adversity or opposing forces. To counter this kind of thinking a leader will have to be entirely committed to a faith approach. That will mean remaining entirely unconcerned by the winds of adversity. Paul is not worried about the snake.

Notice how rapidly the opinions of the crowd change. As soon as Paul did not keel over and die, the crowd entirely reversed its assessment and Paul was suddenly a god in their eyes. Transitional leaders simply must find a way to be immune to the anxieties of crowd opinion.

Beyond all expectation the passengers all survived and eventually made it to their destination. Perhaps the greatest value a transitional leader can provide is that calm assurance that is constantly telling everyone, "We will get to the destination."

The value of this shipwreck narrative is far greater than any bulleted list of leadership points. It may help to return to this narrative from time to time in an effort to appropriate the deep images of leadership projected by Paul. Many forms of shipwreck may present themselves and the deepest impulses of Paul will emerge in your interactions once you have absorbed this narrative.

I was recently watching a movie about the racehorse Secretariat. As a child I had watched the Belmont stakes live when Secretariat won the third leg of the Triple Crown by thirty-one lengths. I vividly remember that astonishing gap between the winning horse and all the rest. So when the movie was building toward the climax, as the story of the week before the race was being told, I was not in any kind of suspense at all. I knew what was going to happen.

Faith does not give us that kind of a window on events, as though we were watching a movie about events we have already seen. But we do have the complete assurance, by faith, that God is in control of events. In commenting on this shipwreck in the book of Acts, Bruce Larson wrote, "God has assured us we're going to come through, somehow, some way. The course may be difficult and fraught with hardships, but ultimately we're going to make it."[1]

Paul's experiences are recorded to build our faith. We are going to make it. But how? In what condition? A transitional pastor's challenge is to lead through the storms and come to the new land with a deeper sense of faith, a greater heart of love, and a more passionate commitment to the mission of the Jesus Christ in the world.

---

1. Larson, *Wind and Fire*, 160.

12

Time to Say Goodbye

John Calvin was sick for most of his adult life. In the last few months of his life he knew he was near the end so he used what strength he had left to finish well. Theodore Beza records three main final acts. On the 25th of April, 1564, he dictated his final will and testament. The document runs to four pages in print. Calvin spent the first half of those pages narrating his inward sense of un-worthiness. To us, in our days of confusion regarding self-esteem, these words may sound unnecessarily bleak. Yet Calvin wanted no shred of false self-confidence to intrude on the plain narration of his total and endless gratitude for being swept up in the goodness of God. He concluded that opening section of confession with these words.

> "But woe is me! my ardour and zeal (if indeed worthy of the name) have been so careless and languid, that I confess I have failed innumerable times to execute my office properly and had not He, of his boundless good-ness, assisted me, all that zeal had been fleeting and vain ... I trust to no other security for my salvation than this, and this only, ... that as God is a Father of mercy, he

will show himself such a Father to me, who acknowledge myself to be a miserable sinner."[1]

Calvin's second act of saying goodbye followed. All of the leaders of the civil government for the city of Geneva were gathered to hear him. Again in humility he spoke of his shortcomings. He thanked them for " . . . having borne patiently with my vehemence, which was sometimes carried to excess;" And then he pointed them to what he taught and what he preached. " . . . I declare that Word of God, entrusted to me, I have taught, not rashly or uncertainly, but purely and sincerely;"[2] He then recapped all they had been through and sealed on their memory the importance of retaining the advances made through gratitude and diligence.

Calvin's third act of goodbye came when the ministers of the city gathered at his bedside. In terms comparable to the peripatetic section of a Pauline epistle, Calvin walked them through a remembrance of all of the greatest battles they had experienced together in the effort to reconstruct the city of Geneva's entire spiritual and social life. Humble to the end, Calvin apologized for his mood during the previous months as he grew sicker and sicker. On the 27th of May, 1564, he died. As Beza put it, "On that day, then, at the same time with the setting sun, this splendid luminary was withdrawn from us" (Beza, *Calvin*, xcvi).

By his own request in his will, Calvin was buried in an unmarked grave in the Geneva cemetery. He was enough aware of his own importance to the world to understand that masses of people would forever be tempted make pilgrimages to his grave like a venerated saint. He was enough aware of that foolishness to request an unknown and unmarked location as his waiting spot for the resurrection.

Many elements for a good goodbye are present in the record we have of Calvin's final goodbye. Walk through these with me and picture the significant ways you can incorporate these elements into your goodbye.

1. Beza, *The Life of John Calvin*, lxxxvii.
2. Ibid., xc.

Intentionally meet with the individuals and circles of people who have meant the most to you. Calvin's choices for how to say goodbye included making intentional statements of thanks to those who had worked with him over the years. Each of these interactions is marked by humility and an effort to drive a deep sense of forgiveness into the ground of these relationships. It is important to face the unfortunate episodes, the mistakes, and the misspoken words. But the failures do not define the relationships.

Surround the past with gratitude. We usually regard the past as a fixed thing, a series of events forever locked in time. Honesty compels us to accept whatever has happened. Yet while events cannot be changed for what they truly were, gratitude can revise what those events truly mean. As you remember what happened you can speak your gratitude and the memories will be transformed by God's grace. In one church I served the personnel committee was subjected to some very difficult challenges. As months went by and we would meet to deal with one unexpected disaster after another, we wondered at the steady flow of bad events. By the time I was saying goodbye to that group their faces represented for me all of the unexpected troubles of the church's transition. Yet I could genuinely feel an ocean of gratitude to these people. Before we met for our last meeting I made a list of things for which I was grateful. We opened and closed each meeting in prayer, and I was grateful for what I learned about God by listening to how those people prayed. Each member of the committee was uniquely equipped by experiences from their past to meet the unusual set of challenges that came our way in those two years and I was grateful for getting to see how God arranges things to walk us through our troubles. As we all spoke words of gratitude in our last meeting together, the rough road of our recent past was transformed.

Take time to meet with individuals who have grown close to you. In this regard, Calvin's example may not be the best. He almost missed an important opportunity to say goodbye to a friend. One of Calvin's greatest friends was William Farel. Years earlier, when Calvin published his commentary on Paul's epistle to Titus, he dedicated it to William Farel, along with another good friend,

Peter Viret. At the time Calvin wrote, "I think that there has never been, in ordinary life, a circle of friends so sincerely bound to each other as we have been in our ministry."[3]

When Calvin was in his last days, word of that sad reality reached his old friend, William Farel. Farel lived in Neufchatel, which was close to eighty miles away from Geneva, where Calvin lay dying. So Farel wrote to Calvin and announced he was coming for a visit. Now Farel was twenty-five years older than Calvin, going on eighty years old, and he was not in the best of health himself. So Calvin sent a letter back to Farel in Neufchatel full of heartfelt words about their friendship, but also telling Farel not to go to the trouble of visiting. Farel came anyway. The two spent a day together and Farel returned to Neufchatel the next day.[4] It may be that Calvin was simply trying to relieve Farel from any burden of guilt if he had not been up to the trip. At any rate, the importance of getting together with friends and spending time together to say goodbye occupies a large place in the ending period of a transitional pastor.

The end of a period of transitional leadership is all about pointing toward the all-encompassing ocean of God's goodness.

For a person charged with leading a church through a transition, your finish line is the congregation's new starting line. This is just one more way that a transitional leader experiences everything as an inversion of what the congregation experiences. Your beginning with them comes when they are emotionally locked into the end of a previous leader's time. This inversion—this sense of opposite focus—persists. Your ending is now their beginning.

When I was a few months away from the end of my first experience I could see one day, in a flash of inspiration, the whole two years in a series of progressive snapshots. I quickly grabbed a pad of paper and a pen and jotted this down. I captured each era mini-era of my time with them with a single sentence. I have gone back now and elaborated on those sentences to explain what each of those sentences meant to me.

3. Calvin, *Commentaries on the Epistle to Titus*, 276.
4. Beza, *Life of Calvin*, xciv.

Interim Pastor Ministry

I Can Help You Know Just What To Do. I started with an optimism that I could lead. I may have been too quick to make decisions in the beginning. Listening a little bit more would have been helpful. At the same time, everyone in the congregation was doing the same with me. A tendency to minimize the impact of the transition meant people spent a lot of time telling me how to do things based on the past.

Sorry You Will Be Leaving So Soon. As time went on we moved into a phase where people were beginning to like what was happening, but they were still eager for me to move along. Due to the discomfort of uncertainty and the reality that my presence was a sign of that uncertainty, people were ready for the transition to be over.

Problem, What Problem? Pastors have ways of suppressing the visibility of problems. In the absence of those patterns of suppression, as problems grew visible, people wanted to believe that the problems would go away as soon as another pastor would come along to help suppress the visibility.

Why Does This Just Keep Happening To Us? Painful events grow out of underlying problems in a congregation. People who are hoping problems will gracefully fade away are repeatedly surprised when an ongoing problem continues to produce painful results in how people are relating to each other. With changes going on in the emotional system of the congregation it is not obvious whether problems are the result of anxiety over the leadership uncertainty or if these painful interactions point to enduring problems.

Someone Needs To Do Something About This. As people acknowledge the reality of enduring problems they may be brave enough to speak the truth about what they are seeing. At this stage they may only speak up if they believe the problems can be solved and if they do not expect to be the one who has to initiate action in order to address the issues

This Is Who We Aspire To Be. At some point a vision of the core identity of the congregation begins to emerge, moving people toward more of an outward focus of mission.

To Be Quite Honest, There Is A Problem. In my experience, the emerging sense of identity and mission creates a safe space for people to identify enduring problems honestly. If things are progressing well, this sense of honesty is accompanied by the courage to take responsibility for the actions necessary to address enduring problems.

One Last Thing Before I Leave. As I could sense I was near the end of my time a sense of urgency and focus gripped my mind. Many things were left undone, but time constraints dictated that those things would remain undone. I prayerfully addressed my energy toward one question: *what one thing can I do before I go for the sake of a smooth transition for the next pastor?* The content of my answer to that question is not significant. Yet it was important to work intentionally all of the way to the finish line.

Let Me Introduce Your New Pastor. In every visible way your support of the next pastor should be readily apparent as the congregation meets him or her for the first time.

Goodbye Saying goodbye well requires a high level of comfort with interpersonal intimacy. Preparing for the day of saying goodbye means reviewing the dynamics of emotional intimacy. It is a challenge to be open enough to people to receive their glowing praise while also having good enough emotional boundaries to resist any of the surreptitious ways that unhealthy people might want to get in one last punch.

Watching From A Distance Pastoral ethics require a separation from the congregation for the sake of allowing the next pastor space to get fully established. While examples of the violation of this basic ethical standard may be routine, make a personal commitment to follow clear guidelines for separation. Make sure people know you are staying away because it is the right thing to do, and that you will still miss them. I recommend a written separation agreement.

I walked together with my first transitional congregation as we faced each event. And then, before I had a moment to reflect on that experience, almost as quickly as I said goodbye to that congregation, Annie and I were immersed in the beginning stages over again with our second congregation in transition. I set the notepad aside. All of the presenting problems in the second congregation felt completely different from what I faced in the first congregation. When we neared the end of that second two-year odyssey I suggested to the leadership team that they should conduct an exit interview with us. As I prepared for that meeting I came across the pad of paper with those eleven stages from my previous congregation. As I read through the points I was very surprised by how similar the stages were, even though the experiences of the two churches were vastly different. Might it be that every human community moves through similar developmental stages as they make a transition?

Within the flow of events, the most important changes came when the congregation accepted its own flaws while still holding onto a vision of what they aspire to be. This may not happen for everyone at once.

As the people begin to perceive that the time of transition is definitely coming to an end they begin to have the capacity to reflect on what they are going through. This turning point is the beginning of the goodbye. While in the beginning they may have been hesitant to truly embrace you as their pastor, suddenly they may begin to perceive the loss that will come when they get what they have always wanted: a new pastor.

As their feelings are changing, as they are expressing regret that you will be leaving, you may already be preparing emotionally for the next thing in your life to begin. You must fight the tendency for your attention and your imagination to drift away from these people. Do not peter out as you approach the finish line. The way they say goodbye to you, and the way that you interact with those genuine expressions of love and gratitude will have an enduring effect on how this congregation handles change in the future.

All of the time you have been measuring your success in various ways. You may have rescued them from administrative mistakes, or you may have created better relationships on the staff. You may have brought new people into the church who are excited about where the congregation is headed, or you may have simply stemmed the membership decline to the best of your ability. However you evaluate your efforts, consider how the best measure of your work will only be apparent years in the future. If you have led this transition well then they are a group of people who calmly trust that God is in control even when they go through difficult losses. The community will be filled with more emotionally and spiritually mature people than it had before. Anxiety will be reduced, not because the road is smoother, but because people will not panic when change is thrust upon them. They have seen change, and they know God can get them through it. Your leadership will have caused them to trust pastors more, but, ironically, to put less of their trust in exactly who that person is. They will have more of a biblical sense of their congregation as a body because Jesus Christ will be at the head and not their pastor.

Saying goodbye is important because your leaving represents the true ending of the previous pastor's ministry. With you there in a temporary leadership capacity people often made reference to his or her leadership. And while people accepted you as their situational pastor, you never replaced the previous pastor in their hearts and minds. To allow you to replace that pastor would have felt like disloyalty. But if you have done your job well your goodbye puts all of that to rest. They will feel it is time to live in this new land with a new pastor as their leader.

And now it is time for me to say goodbye to you. The writing of this book felt like the work of a blacksmith. I searched for the raw materials, outlined the basic shape, then hammered, ground and honed to create an implement for your service. You have been on my mind all of the while. I know you will be subjected to some hammering, grinding, and honing while you walk with people from the land of loss to a new place under new pastoral leadership. It will be very rewarding. I have thank you gifts from each of my transitional congregations that I will keep all of my life and pass down to my children. But it may not be rewarding in the way you were hoping. And some of the sacrifices will not be—cannot be—compensated. I have spent this time with you, walking with you into a new land, because over the many years of my life a few moments of health in some really good congregations contributed immeasurably to my spiritual growth. And even though churches may tend to be a mess these days, I still believe healthy congregations can emerge from the troubles we see around us. And I believe the blank space between pastors is one of the best places to begin moving toward that health.

Bibliography

Beza, Theodore. *The Life of John Calvin*, in *Selected Works of John Calvin: Tracts and Letters*, Beveridge, Henry and Bonnet, Jules, eds. V. 1, Tracts, Part 1. Grand Rapids, Michigan: Baker, 1983. A reproduction of *Tracts, vol. 1, Relating to the Reformation*. Edinburgh: Calvin Translation Society, 1844.

Calvin, John. *Commentaries on the Epistle to Titus*. Pringle, William Trans. Grand Rapids, MI: Baker Book House. In *Commentaries on the Epistles to Timothy, Titus, and Philemon*. (Baker). Calvin's Commentaries 22-Volume Set, originally printed for the Calvin Translation Society, Edinburgh, 1854. Reprinted by Baker, 1996.

Doenecke, Justus D. *The Presidencies of James A. Garfield & Chester A. Arthur*. Lawrence, Kansas: The Regents Press of Kansas. American Presidency Series. 1981.

Edwards, James R. *The Gospel According to Mark*. The Pillar New Testament Commentary. Grand Rapids, Michigan: Eerdmans, 2002.

Flippen, Flip. *The Flip Side: Break Free of the Behaviors That Hold You Back*. New York: Springboard, 2007.

Hayner, Stephen Allen. "Suffering and the Prophetic Vocation." PhD diss., University of Saint Andrews, Scotland, http://hdl.handle. net/10023/2813,1984.

Heifetz, Ronald, Grashow, Alexander and Linksy, Marty. *The Practice of Adaptive Leadership: Tools and Tactics for Changing Your Organization and the World*. Boston: Harvard Business, 2009.

Jacobs, Alan. *The Narnian*. New York: HarperCollins, 2005.

Larson, Bruce. *The Meaning and Mystery of Being Human*. Waco, Texas: Word, 1978.

———. *Wind & Fire: Living Out the Book of Acts*. Waco, Texas: Word, 1984.

Lewis, C.S. *The Voyage of the Dawn Treader*. First published by Geoffrey Bles, 1952. Reprinted in Middlesex, England: Puffin, 1965.

Lossing, Benson John. *A Biography of James A. Garfield*. New York: H.S. Goodspeed & Co.,1882.

Munger, Robert Boyd, and Larson, Robert C. *Leading from the Heart: Lifetime Reflections on Spiritual Development*. Downers Grove, IL: InterVarsity, 1995.

Bibliography

Rediger, G. Lloyd. *Clergy Killers: Guidance for Pastors and Congregations Under Attack*. Louisville, Kentucky: Westminster John Knox, 1997.

Richardson, Ronald W. *Family Ties That Bind: A Self-Help Guide To Change Through Family of Origin Therapy*, 2nd ed. Vancouver, B. C.: International Self-Counsel, 1987.

Steinke, Peter L. *How Your Church Family Works: Understanding Congregations As Emotional Systems*. Herndon, Virginia: The Alban Institute, 1993.

Tolkien, J. R. R. "On Fairy-Stories," in *Essays Presented to Charles Williams*, C. S. Lewis, ed., 38–89. Oxford: Oxford University Press, 1947; Grand Rapids, Michigan: Eerdmans, 1966.

Zimmerman, Richard P. "The Fiction That Helps Us To Live." ThM Thesis, Regent College, 1995.